A Typological Study of Evidentiality in Qiangic Languages

Linguistics

Volumes published in this Brill Research Perspectives title are listed at *brill.com/rplis*

A Typological Study of Evidentiality in Qiangic Languages

By

Junwei Bai

BRILL

LEIDEN | BOSTON

Library of Congress Control Number: 2022915749

Typeface for the Latin, Greek, and Cyrillic scripts: "Brill". See and download: brill.com/brill-typeface.

ISSN 2667-0682
ISBN 978-90-04-52626-6 (paperback)
ISBN 978-90-04-52628-0 (e-book)

Copyright 2022 by Junwei Bai. Published by Koninklijke Brill NV, Leiden, The Netherlands.
Koninklijke Brill NV incorporates the imprints Brill, Brill Nijhoff, Brill Hotei, Brill Schöningh, Brill Fink, Brill mentis, Vandenhoeck & Ruprecht, Böhlau and V&R unipress.
Koninklijke Brill NV reserves the right to protect this publication against unauthorized use. Requests for re-use and/or translations must be addressed to Koninklijke Brill NV via brill.com or copyright.com.

This book is printed on acid-free paper and produced in a sustainable manner.

Contents

    Abbreviations   VII
    Abstract   1
    Keywords   1
1 Introduction   1
    1.1 *Two Approaches to Evidentiality*   1
    1.2 *The Qiangic Branch*   3
    1.3 *Framework, Concepts and Terminologies*   6
        1.3.1 Framework of Analysis   6
        1.3.2 Volitional and Non-volitional Verbs   8
        1.3.3 Endopathic Verbs   8
        1.3.4 Egophoric, or Egophoricity   8
        1.3.5 Mirativity and Mirative Extensions of Evidentials   9
        1.3.6 First-Person Effects   9
        1.3.7 Language, Dialect and Variety   10
    1.4 *Treatment of Sources*   10
2 Evidentiality in Qiangic Languages   11
    2.1 *Core Rgyalrong*   11
        2.1.1 Cogtse Variety   12
        2.1.2 Jiaomuzu Variety   15
        2.1.3 Japhug Dialect   19
    2.2 *Khroskyabs*   23
    2.3 *Horpa*   26
        2.3.1 Rtau Variety   26
        2.3.2 Geshiza Variety   27
    2.4 *Qiang*   30
        2.4.1 Ronghong Variety   30
        2.4.2 Qugu Variety   33
        2.4.3 Puxi Variety   38
        2.4.4 Longxi Variety   39
    2.5 *nDrapa*   40
        2.5.1 Upper Dialect   40
        2.5.2 Lower Dialect   43
    2.6 *Munya*   45
    2.7 *Ersu*   49
        2.7.1 Ersu Proper   49
        2.7.2 Lizu Dialect   52

2.8　*Pumi*　53
　　　　2.8.1　Southern Dialect　53
　　　　2.8.2　Northern Dialect　54
　　2.9　*Guiqiong*　57
　　2.10　*Shixing*　59
3　Discussion　60
　　3.1　*Three Types of Evidentiality Systems*　60
　　3.2　*Evidentiality in Qiangic: Genetic Retention or Independent Development?*　60
　　3.3　*Theoretical Implications*　66
　　　　3.3.1　The Special Properties of the Direct Evidential　66
　　　　3.3.2　Grammaticalization of the Reported and Quotative Evidentials　69
4　Summary　70
　　References　70
　　Index　76

Abbreviations

1	first person
2	second person
3	third person
ASP.NEG	aspectual negator
ASR	assertive
ATT	speaker attitude marker
CAUS	causative
CL	classifier
CLF	classifier
CLF:GENR	general classifier
CLF:LONG	classifier for long objects
CLF:MAN	classifier for human
CON	continuative aspect
CONJ	conjunction
CONTR	negative contrastive marker
COP	copula
CS	cislocative direction
CSM	change of state marker
DAT	dative
DEEXP	de-experiencer
DEF	definite
DEM	demonstrative
DISJ	disjunct
DOWN	downward direction
DS	downstream direction
DSC	discourse clitic
DU	dual
EGO	egophoricity
EMPH	emphatic
ERG	ergative
EVID:ASU	assumed evidential
EVID:AUD	auditory evidential
EVID:DIRECT	direct evidential
EVID:EREP	experienced reported evidential
EVID:FACTUAL	factual evidential
EVID:FH	firsthand evidential

EVID:GREP	gnomic reported evidential
EVID:INFR	inferential evidential
EVID:NFH	non-firsthand evidential
EVID:OBS	observational evidential
EVID:PRE	predictive evidential
EVID:QUO	quotative evidential
EVID:REP	reported evidential
EVID:VIS	visual evidential
EXCL	exclusive
EXCLAM	exclamatory
EXP	experiencer case
FACT	factual
FOC	focus
FRM	frame setter
FUT	future
GEN	genitive
GN	gnomic tense
HET	heterophoric
IMM	immediate aspect
IMPF	imperfective
IN	inward direction
INCL	inclusive
INDEF	indefinite
INS	instrumental
INTERJ	interjection
INTRG	interrogative
INV	inverse
LNK	linker
LOC	locative
LOG	logophoric
MOD	modal discourse enclitic
NEG	negative
NMLZ	nominalizer
NOM	nominative
NON.CTRL	non-control
NON.EGO	non-egophoric
NON.EXPR	non-experiential mood
NON.FIN	non-finite
NON.PST	non-past

ABBREVIATIONS

NONS	non-specific direction
OUT	outward direction
PFV	perfective
PL	plural
PN	proper noun
POSS	possessive
PREST	present speaker
PROG	progressive
PROS	prospective
PRS	present
PST	past
REC	reciprocity marker
REDU	reduplicated form
REL	relative
SBJ	subject
SFP	sentence-final particle
SG	singular
SLF	first person self (narrator)
STA	stative aspect
SUPRESS	superessive
TOP	topic
TS	translocative direction
UP	upward direction
US	upstream direction
V	verb citation
VOC	vocative
VOL	volitive

A Typological Study of Evidentiality in Qiangic Languages

Junwei Bai
Adjunct Fellow of The College of Arts, Society, and Education,
James Cook University, Cairns, Australia
junwei.bai@my.jcu.edu.au

Abstract

This study looks at the grammatical category of evidentiality in Qiangic languages within the typological framework developed by Aikhenvald. An examination of nine Qiangic languages, with a total of sixteen dialects and varieties, shows that the evidential systems currently identified can be grouped into three categories: the Rgyalrongic type, which is characterized by a firsthand and a non-firsthand subsystem in the past tense, the Qiang type, with a visual, an inferential, and a reported evidential, and the southern Qiangic type, which consists of a direct, an inferential, and a reported and/or a quotative evidential. After comparing these systems, it is found that there is little or no conclusive evidence for them to be inherited from a proto-language, instead, they are more likely to have developed independently. The special properties of the direct evidentials and the unusual composition of the reported and quotative evidentials recurrent in several languages are also discussed.

Keywords

Tibeto-Burman – Trans-Himalayan – Qiang – Sichuan – China – rGyalrong/Gyalrong/Rgyalrong – Muya/Munya/Minyag – Ersu – nDrapa – Pumi/Prinmi – Khroskyabs – Horpa – Evidentiality – Typology

1   Introduction

1.1   *Two Approaches to Evidentiality*

In theory and practice, two main approaches to evidentiality are currently followed by Tibeto-Burmanists. One approach understands evidentiality to be the grammatical encoding of the source of information (e.g. J. T.-S. Sun 1993; LaPolla 2003; Lidz 2007; Willis 2007: 504; Widmer 2014: 538; Watters 2018: 501;

DeLancey 2018; Hyslop 2018). This has also been the standard characterization of evidentiality from the typological perspective (e.g. Chafe and Nichols 1986; Willett 1988; Aikhenvald and Dixon 2003; Aikhenvald 2004, 2015, 2018; San Roque, Floyd, and Norcliffe 2017). Another approach, which arose relatively recently and is meant to cover a broader range of phenomena, views evidentiality as 'the representation of source and access to information according to the speaker's perspective and strategy' (Tournadre and LaPolla 2014). In this definition, 'source' means 'primarily a verbal source of information (reported information)' and 'access' is characterized as 'the non-verbal access to information (sensory, inferential, etc., including the sensory access to verbal source) available to the speaker'. The second approach seems to be primarily inspired by works on Tibetic languages and dialects, and is now mostly followed by Tibetanists (e.g. Tournadre and Jiatso 2001; Oisel 2017; Hill and Gawne 2017; Gawne 2017; Yliniemi 2019: 257), and to a lesser extent, researchers who work on Qiangic languages (e.g. J. T.-S. Sun 2018, 2019b; Jacques 2019).

The two approaches are largely congruent. To be specific, the 'source of information' as defined in the second approach corresponds to the reported evidential or the quotative evidential in the first approach, and the types of 'non-verbal access to information' overlap to a great deal with other categories recognized in the first formulation, such as visual evidential, non-visual sensory evidential, inferential evidential, and so on.

However, one major disparity between the two lines of research lies in the treatment of egophoric, which, according to Tournadre and LaPolla (2014), denotes the sense of self-awareness or personal knowledge. The second approach sees egophoric as a kind of evidential category, and calls it 'egophoric evidential' (Tournadre and LaPolla 2014) or 'personal evidential' (Hill and Gawne 2017). Whereas in the first approach, egophoric is not seen as a type of evidential, but as an independent grammatical category, though the two can be intertwined in some languages. The nature of this connection can be unraveled if we take a broader perspective, and subsume evidentiality, together with egophoricity, mirativity, and modality, under the more encompassing grammatical category of knowledge expression. Thus, evidentiality pertains to the grammatical expression of information source, egophoricity is the grammatical expression of access to knowledge, mirativity is the encoding of expectations of knowledge, and (epistemic) modality is how grammar expresses attitude to knowledge (Aikhenvald 2014, 2018, 2021).

This study will take the first approach, for two reasons. Firstly, as is demonstrated by Aikhenvald (2021), while the four categories of knowledge expression as mentioned above can be interconnected in many ways, the demarcations among them can nevertheless be maintained. In particular, cross-linguistically, evidentiality exhibits properties which are not shared by the other three categories, such as functional scope, possibility of double marking, time reference being different from that of the predicate, the option of being negated or questioned separately from the predicate of the clause, and specific correlations with speech genres and social environment. Thus a distinction between evidentiality and egophoricity is warranted. Secondly, recently there is an emerging trend to treat egophoricity as a cross-linguistically valid grammatical category (e.g. Floyd, Norcliffe, and San Roque 2018; Hyslop 2018). The first approach is more coherent with this trend and, compared with the second approach, allows for more in-depth and thorough study of egophoricity in the future.

The aim of this study is to survey the evidential systems of declarative main clauses in Qiangic languages from a typological perspective. The remainder of this thesis is structured as follows. The necessary preliminaries will be laid out in §1.2, which is a brief introduction to Qiangic languages, and §1.3, which outlines the analytic framework and defines and clarifies key terminologies. The body of this study, §2, will present the evidential systems reported in different Qiangic language, starting from Rgyalrongic languages in the north (§2.1–§2.3), followed by Qiang (§2.4), nDrapa (§2.5) and Munya (§2.6) in the middle area, and ends with Ersu (§2.7), Pumi (§2.8) and Guiqiong (§2.9) in the south. The third part will first categorize the evidentiality systems found in these languages (§3.1), then discuss whether these systems have a common origin or arose independently in each language (§3.2). Two typologically unusual features found in Qiangic languages will also be highlighted (§3.3), one concerning the direct evidential (§3.3.1), the other the reported and/or quotative evidential (§3.3.2). The last section (§4) summarizes this study.

1.2 *The Qiangic Branch*

As a language group in the Tibeto-Burman language family, the validity of the Qiangic branch has gained wide acceptance, though there are still some disputes. The proposal to set up this branch was first made by H. K. Sun (1962), and subsequently expounded in many of his writings, notably H. K. Sun (1983) and H. K. Sun (2016). The most recent classification by Sun includes thirteen Qiangic languages, which are given in Figure 1.1.

There are three levels in this phylogeny. On the first level, the languages are divided into three sub-branches based on their geographical distribution, which are the Northern sub-branch, the Middle sub-branch and the Southern sub-branch. Each sub-branch further contains one to three groups, and each

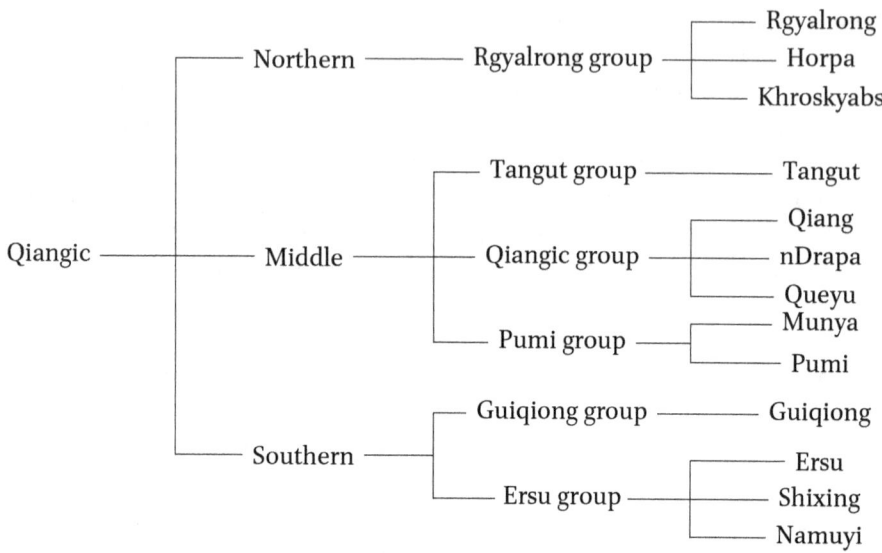

FIGURE 1.1   The phylogeny of Qiangic languages
ADAPTED FROM H. K. SUN 2016: 4

group consists of one to three languages. Almost all these languages have dialects, the number of which varies depending on their distribution and vitality. Tangut has died for a long time, and many other languages are critically endangered, particularly those in the middle and the southern sub-branch.

Qiangic languages are mostly spoken in the western part of Sichuan province in China, where the main topography features high mountains and deep valleys, with farming-conducive parcels of land dispersed here and there in dales. The distribution of these languages are shown in Map 1.1. Except for speakers of Qiang and Pumi, who are officially recognized as an independent ethnic group, other speakers of Qiangic languages are identified as subgroups of Tibetans. Speakers of this language are heavily influenced by Tibetan languages and culture in the north and west and Chinese languages and culture in the east and south. Roughly speaking, the languages spoken in the north are varieties of Amdo Tibetan and those in the west are dialects of Kham Tibetan. The Chinese languages that are in contact with Qiangic languages in the south and east are mostly Mandarin Chinese and Southwestern Mandarin.

Qiangic languages are similar in many respects but also exhibit considerable variations. In terms of commonalities, they tend to have a large inventory of consonants and vowels. Tones generally carry a very low functional load, and tend to be marked on phonological words instead of syllables. Pronouns have three numbers: Singular, dual and plural, with the inclusive-exclusive distinction made in first person dual and plural. Nouns can take numeral classifiers or

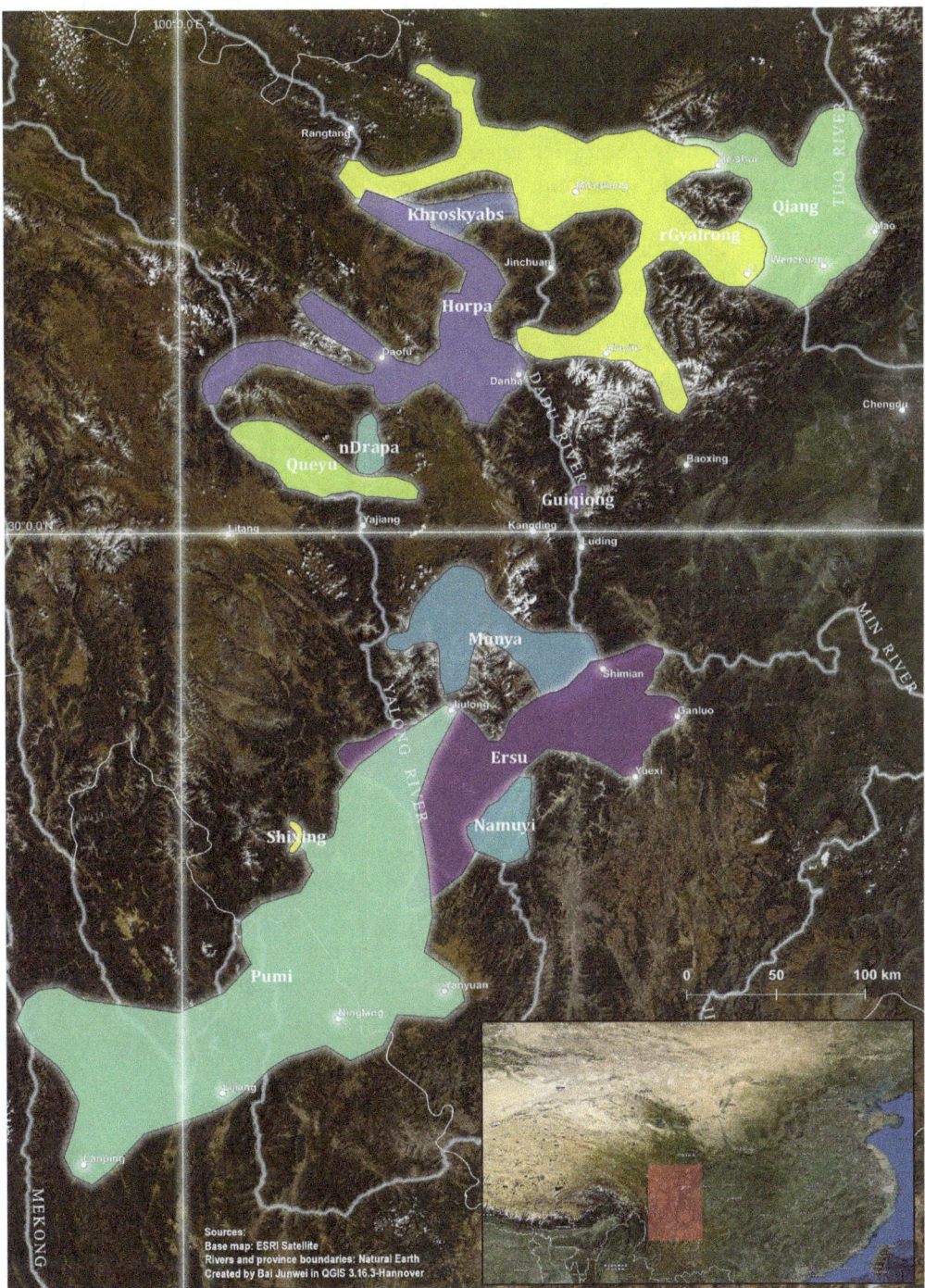

MAP 1.1 The geographical distribution of Qiangic languages
MAP CREATED BY JUNWEI BAI

be marked with non-obligatory plural markers. Verbs generally take directional prefixes, which, aside from marking direction, can denote perfectivity or commands in some languages. Most languages index person-number information on verbs, either with suffixation, as in Rgyalrong languages, or through vocalic change, as in Munya. Many languages have the reciprocal category, multiple existential verbs and a wide range of case markers. And, as will be shown in this study, evidentiality is also prevalent, found in almost all sufficiently described languages, though the organization of these systems can vary from language to language. [For a more comprehensive list of the commonalities in Qiangic languages, see H. K. Sun (2016: 9–15) and Chirkova (2012).]

With regards to variations, northern Qiangic languages are generally more complex in phonology and morphology than members in the middle or south. For example, the languages within the Rgyalrong group, and, to a lesser extent, the Qiang group, tend to have a large number of initial consonant clusters. According to Lai (2017: 100), Khroskyabs boasts 715 such clusters, which is by far the largest inventory among Tibeto-Burman languages. Such clusters have either been radically simplified or completely lost in middle and southern languages. In Munya, no such cluster is identified, with only prenasalized consonants optionally analyzable in this way (Bai 2019: 41). As for morphology, Rgyalrong languages are highly agglutinative and predominantly prefixal, and can have over ten types of prefixes in the verb template (Jacques 2008; J. T.-S. Sun 2017; Nagano 2017). In contrast, verb roots in the middle and southern Qiangic languages generally only take the directional prefix, the negative prefix, and the interrogative prefix.

1.3 *Framework, Concepts and Terminologies*

This section introduces the analytic framework adopted in this study, as well as the key concepts and terminologies that have a bearing on understanding how evidentiality works in Qiangic languages. The framework outlined in §1.3.1 is based on Aikhenvald (2004, 2015, 2018), and the concepts to be introduced include volitionality (§1.3.2), endopathic verbs (§1.3.3), egophoricity (§1.3.4), mirativity (§1.3.5) and first-person effects (§1.3.6).

1.3.1   Framework of Analysis

Aikhenvald (2004: 63–4) establishes six semantic parameters that are commonly employed by languages with grammatical evidentiality across the world, covering physical senses and several types of inference and verbal report. An important parameter in many Tibetic and Qiangic languages is ENDOPATHIC, which is the hallmark of the direct evidential. For the purpose of this study, it is added to the inventory of well-established parameters, as type iii. Thus there are seven major semantic parameters that are covered by evidentials in Qiangic languages, which are given below.

(I)   VISUAL covers information acquired through seeing;
(II) SENSORY covers information obtained through hearing, smelling, tasting and touching.
(III) ENDOPATHIC covers bodily and internal feelings and experiences, such as cold, pain, hunger, illness, desire, yearn, as well as emotions such as fear and anger.
(IV) INFERENCE is based on visible or tangible result;
(V)   ASSUMPTION is based on information other than visible results: this may include logical reasoning, assumption or simply general knowledge;
(VI) REPORTED, for reported information with no reference to who it was reported by;
(VII) QUOTATIVE, for reported information with an overt reference to the authorship of the quoted source.

Languages vary in how they group the recurrent semantic parameters within their evidential systems. Cross-linguistically, the most straightforward grouping is found in three-term systems where sensory parameters (I and II), inference and assumption (IV and V), and reported and quotative (VI and VII) are each grouped together. Languages with a binary system generally have a firsthand evidential covering i or i and ii, and a non-firsthand evidential covering the rest. Languages with four or more choices tend to distinguish between a reported evidential (covered by VI) and a quotative evidential (covered by VII), or have separate terms for the inferential evidential (IV) and the assumed evidential (V). For a more comprehensive discussion on the types and variations in the grouping patterns, see Aikhenvald (2004: 63–6).

Evidentiality may correlate with other categories, such as person, the tense system, the aspect system, sentence types, polarity, modality, and egophoricity. One important aspect of this correlation is that there can be more than one evidentiality systems in one language, and the choice of a subsystem may depend on a choice made in the tense system or in the mood system. As will be shown in this study, Rgyalrong languages tend to have a firsthand evidential and a non-firsthand evidential in the past tense and a different system in non-past tenses. The choice of an evidential can also be jointly determined by other semantic, pragmatic or grammatical factors. For example, certain evidentials in Qiangic languages interact with person, volitionality of predicate, and sentence types (declarative or interrogative).

Exponents of evidentiality may develop additional overtones. For example, in two-term systems, the firsthand evidential may have overtones of the speaker's control and participation. In larger systems, the visual evidential marker may acquire overtones of certainty and refer to 'generally observable facts'. The inferential evidential may acquire overtones of doubt or speculation, and show first-person effects when used with first person subjects.

An evidential can be expressed autonomously, with a dedicated marker, or it can be fused with another category. In the overwhelming number of examples of fused evidentiality, evidentiality is fused with tense or with aspect. An evidential can also be formally unmarked. In many cases, the least formally marked verb in a language with evidentiality tends to acquire a visual, or a firsthand reading. This is the case of many varieties of Rgyalrong and Qiang.

1.3.2   Volitional and Non-volitional Verbs

It has long been noticed that in Tibeto-Burman languages the semantic parameter of volitionality (also termed as 'control' or 'controllability') in verbal predicates can have a strong influence on different facets of the grammar (e.g. Hale 1980; DeLancey 1986; J. T.-S. Sun 1993; Tournadre and Jiatso 2001; Hargreaves 2005; Daudey 2014b; Bai 2019: 91), particularly evidentiality. Generally speaking, a volitional verb means a verb which denotes actions that normally can be consciously initiated or be performed with awareness by the actor, while a non-volitional verb means a verb which refers to actions that normally cannot be exercised under conscious control or with intention.

1.3.3   Endopathic Verbs

The term 'endopathic' was coined by Tournadre (1996) and refers to a kind of verb with special lexical semantics. Endopathic verbs denote sensations or internal feelings and experiences, such as cold, pain and hunger, as well as emotions such as fear and anger. In some Qiangic languages, clauses with endopathic predicates can have special requirements on the person of subjects or the use of evidential and egophoric markers. While endopathic verbs are generally non-volitional, the two types do not completely overlap, and for the purpose of this study, endopathic verbs can be seen as a sub-type of non-volitional verbs.

1.3.4   Egophoric, or Egophoricity

There is as yet no consensus on the definition of egophoric or egophoricity.[1] The term 'egophoric' was first proposed by Hagège (1974) (as *égophorique*). It was then borrowed by Tournadre (1992, 2008) and was used to denote personal knowledge or intention on the part of the speaker, and grammatical morphemes with egophoric senses were treated as evidentials. However, some

---

[1] Most scholars use these two terms interchangeably, though Hill and Gawne (2017) believe that 'egophoricity' is a misnomer and only 'egophoric' should be retained.

researchers prefer to treat it as a category independent of evidentiality, such as Post (2013) and Daudey (2014b). Furthermore, there is a recent trend to establish egophoricity as a cross-linguistically valid category (Floyd, Norcliffe, and San Roque 2018). This term is commonly used to refer to speakers' volitional involvement in a situation and access to information (Hyslop 2018; Aikhenvald 2021), where 'access' can mean whether the information is personal or shared by the addressee (Aikhenvald 2021).

1.3.5 Mirativity and Mirative Extensions of Evidentials

Mirativity pertains to the expectation of knowledge (Aikhenvald 2014; Hyslop 2018). The idea of establishing mirativity as a cross-linguistically valid grammatical category was initially put forward by DeLancey (1997). It was substantially developed in Aikhenvald (2012), where sudden discovery, revelation or realization, surprise, counter-expectation, unprepared mind and new information were all included within the range of mirative meanings. Also, the mirative effects are not restricted to the speaker, and can also be on the part of the addressee or a third person.

This is a category in its own right in some languages, but there are also many languages for which certain evidential categories can be extended to express mirative meanings. According to Aikhenvald (2004: 195), in small systems with two evidentials, the non-firsthand evidential can acquire mirative overtones. In larger systems, similar range of meanings can be expressed with the inferential evidential, or occasionally, the reported evidential.

1.3.6 First-Person Effects

It may seem paradoxical to use a non-firsthand or non-visual evidential in a clause where the speaker is reporting about herself, as information of this sort is normally supposed to be direct. However, in many languages this use does occur, and in that case the non-firsthand or non-visual evidential will acquire additional meanings. More specifically, these evidentials would denote that the speaker's actions are non-volitional, or that they are performed without control or awareness. They can also have overtones of unprepared mind, surprise, or new information—in other words, mirativity. The connotations of non-volitionality and non-consciousness which arise from using a non-firsthand, non-visual or reported evidential to make assertions about the speaker herself is called 'first-person effects'[2] (Aikhenvald 2004: 220; J. T.-S. Sun 2018).

---

2 This terminology was first used by Aikhenvald, in a position paper for a workshop on evidentiality held in 2001 (Aikhenvald, personal communication, February 22, 2021). The position paper was later revised and published in Aikhenvald and Dixon (2003), a volume which emanated from that workshop.

1.3.7   Language, Dialect and Variety

Throughout this study, I will use 'language' to refer to the nine Qiangic languages whose evidential systems will be discussed in §2. Some of these languages can have two or more dialects, which may or may not be mutually intelligible. These will be referred to as 'dialects', e.g. the Situ dialect of Rgyalrong. Furthermore, some dialects can have more than one sub-dialects (or sub-sub-dialects), and these will be called 'variety', e.g. the Jiaomuzu variety of the Situ dialect. Since many dialects and varieties are named after the places where they are spoken, in cases where there is no possibility of ambiguity, they will simply be denoted with the place name. For example, the Jiaomuzu variety is sometimes simply referred to as 'Jiaomuzu'.

1.4   *Treatment of Sources*

As was mentioned in §1.1, this study will take evidentiality to be a closed system of grammatical forms whose primary meaning is information source, with the purpose of examining, in this perspective, how evidentiality is manifested and organized in those Qiangic languages that are reported to have such a system. Needless to say, in deciding whether or not a category is evidential in nature, not all researchers of Qiangic languages strictly follow this criterion. Therefore, it is necessary that the data, analyses and conclusions presented in the original sources be scrutinized, evaluated, and if necessary, reorganized or even reanalyzed before they can be meaningfully discussed and compared within the present framework.

The following work has been done to the original sources. Since in this study, egophoricity is not regarded as a type of evidentiality, it is excluded from consideration wherever it is treated within evidentiality systems. Some researchers discuss epistemic modality and other categories whose core function is not information source marking together with evidentiality. Those categories are not regarded as evidentials in this study either. Furthermore, in some reference grammars with a section dedicated to evidentiality, certain evidential categories, such as the reported evidential or some zero-marked evidential, are discussed in the body of that section but left out in the introductory part, because of which some deficient generalizations are arrived at. This has been rectified in this study. Moreover, there is a high degree of inconsistency with respect to the terms chosen by different scholars for certain evidential categories. Following the framework presented in §1.3.1, the terms used in the original sources have been renamed wherever necessary to avoid confusion and facilitate comparison. Finally, while efforts have been made to keep glossings identical to the original analyses as much as possible, all evidential morphemes have been re-glossed for consistency. Also completely re-glossed are verbal directional prefixes, as it occurs so often in example sentences but are glossed wildly inconsistently in different studies.

2   Evidentiality in Qiangic Languages

This section will examine the evidential systems from sixteen dialects and varieties of nine Qiangic languages. These languages are (in order of presentation): Rgyalrong, Khroskyabs, Horpa, Qiang, nDrapa, Munya, Ersu, Pumi, and Guiqiong. Tangut, Queyu and Namuyi are not included in the discussion because as far as I know, no study has thus far been published on the evidential systems in these languages. The situation in Shixing is only briefly mentioned, partly because the language is still poorly understood, partly because there are great controversies on whether or not there are evidentials in this language.

Most of these languages have a reported evidential. Some languages may in addition has a quotative evidential, while for others the reported and quotative evidentials are in the same form. Some prominent features can be observed for different subgroups. For example, in Rgyalrongic languages, evidentiality in the past tense generally bifurcates into an unmarked firsthand category, expressing information obtained from direct sources, and a non-firsthand category, coding information acquired from inference or hearsay. Varieties of Qiang all have a visual evidential, which tends to be optionally marked or simply unmarked. A direct evidential interacting with the person of actors and volitionality is documented for several southern Qiangic languages. Mirative extensions and first-person effects are widely attested, primarily for the non-firsthand and inferential evidentials.

Certain varieties may have their unique evidential categories that are not shared even by other varieties or dialects of the same language. For example, Jiaomuzu Rgyalrong has an observational evidential covering several distantly related functions; Qugu Qiang has a predictive evidential and an assumed evidential; and Wadu Pumi has an auditory evidential which is dedicated to mark information obtained from hearing.

We will now discuss in details the evidentiality in the varieties and dialects of the nine Qiangic languages.

2.1   *Core Rgyalrong*
Rgyalrongic languages can be broadly divided into Core Rgyalrong and the Khroskyabs-Horpa subgroup (J. T.-S. Sun 2000a,b; Jacques 2017). Core Rgyalrong consists of four mutually-unintelligible dialects: Situ, Japhug, Tshobdun and Zbu (a.k.a. Showu), each with many distinct varieties. The

Khroskyabs-Horpa subgroup consists of Khroskyabs (a.k.a. Lavrung) and Horpa (a.k.a. Stau or Ergong).

Conservative Rgyalrongic languages typically have a tripartite tense-aspect system that contrasts a past perfective, a past imperfective, and a non-past imperfective. Aspect is coded with directional prefixes, while tense is expressed with stem alternations (J. T.-S. Sun 2000a,b; Y.-J. Lin 2003; Jacques 2008: 259–300; Tian and J. T.-S. Sun 2019). Evidentiality in Rgyalrongic languages tends to be tightly fused with tense-aspect. In the past tense, there is normally a zero-marked firsthand evidential and a non-firsthand evidential, the latter being formed through vocalic change in directional-cum-tense/aspect prefixes (in many cases to *a*). Most varieties have a reported evidential, and some also have a direct evidential that is restricted to non-past situations. Certain varieties have evidentials not shared by others, such as the observational evidential in Jiaomuzu, the factual evidential in Japhug, and the quotative evidential in Geshiza.

Not all major dialects of this language group have been well documented. For Core Rgyalrong, J. T.-S. Sun (2017) mentions that the Tshobdun evidential system consists basically of a mediative =*cə* and a hearsay =*tétsə*, and the situation in Zbu is currently unknown. Thus only two dialects of Core Rgyalrong will be discussed below, which are Situ (including the Cogtse variety in §2.1.1 and the Jiaomuzu variety in §2.1.2) and Japhug (§2.1.3). As to the Khroskyabs-Horpa subgroup, descriptions on evidentiality are available for Wobzi Khroskyabs (§2.2) and the Rtau (§2.3.1) and Geshiza (§2.3.2) variety of Horpa.

2.1.1 Cogtse Variety

Most studies on Situ Rgyalrong are focused on the Cogtse (a.k.a. Zhuokeji) variety. The grammatical systems with evidential functions are mentioned in X. R. Lin (1993) and Y.-J. Lin (2000), and the system in the first study is adopted here for its greater accessibility.

As with other early works on Qiangic languages, X. R. Lin (1993) does not explicitly discuss evidentiality in Cogtse. Nevertheless, based on his description, it seems that a firsthand and non-firsthand evidential distinction is made in both the past tense and the present tense. According to X. R. Lin (1993: 231–2), Cogtse has a past tense, a present tense, and a future tense,[3] which are marked via verbal prefixes. We will first look at the system in the past tense.

---

3   Different analyses of the tense-aspect system in Cogtse are proposed by Y.-J. Lin (2003) and Nagano (2017). Y.-J. Lin (2003) argues that Cogtse has a tense-aspect system of perfective, imperfective (which further consists of a present tense and a past tense form), prospective

In several places of his work, X. R. Lin (1993: 194–5, 240, 390–1) mentions that when describing past situations, speakers need to formally indicate their epistemic status and information source. Specifically, in non-first person environment, they need to show whether they are familiar with (*shuxi*) or deeply-know (*shenzhi*) or have visual evidence for (*qinjian*) or are certain of (*kending*) the provided information, or only roughly know (*fanzhi*) or have not witnessed (*weiqinjian*) or are uncertain of (*bukending*) the event being characterized. And in first-person environments, speakers need to mark whether the action is carried out volitionally or non-volitionally. For ease of reference, we can label these distinctions as a firsthand evidential (including non-first person familiar and first person volitional cases) versus a non-firsthand evidential (including non-first person unfamiliar and first person non-volitional situations).

This notionally person-sensitive contrast is coded in a binary way in directional prefixes. There are two sets of directional prefixes in Cogtse, one set is used in future and present tense while the other set is used for past tense and imperatives (X. R. Lin 1993: 228). When verb roots take the past tense directional prefixes, the evidential meaning of the clause is firsthand; and to express the non-firsthand senses, the vowels in these prefixes need to be changed to *a* (X. R. Lin 1993: 390).

Compare (1a), a firsthand situation, with (1b), a non-firsthand situation (X. R. Lin 1993: 390).

(1) a. *wəjo jə-pi*
   3SG   NONS+EVID:FH-come
   'He has come.' (The speaker either has witnessed, or is familiar with, or is certain of this event.)

   b. *wəjo ja-po*
   3SG   NONS+EVID:NFH-come
   'He has come.' (The speaker only roughly knows, or is unfamiliar with, or is uncertain of this event.)

---

and non-past, rather than a simplex tripartite tense distinction as put forward in X. R. Lin (1993). And in addition to prefixation, verb stems need to be alternated through ablaut and/or tone and pitch-accent devices in certain tense-aspect categories. While Y.-J. Lin (2003)'s treatment seems to be more comprehensive and can better account for the data, she did not mention the evidential functions of the tense-aspect markers in her study. For the purpose of this study, we still follow X. R. Lin (1993)'s approach.

Similarly, in the following pair of examples, where the participant is the speaker, (2a) indicates that the speaker did his shooting consciously whereas (2b) means the action was carried out without awareness (X. R. Lin 1993: 391).

(2) a. ŋa məʃər ʃamndu to-lan
    1SG yesterday gun UP+EVID:FH-shoot
    'I did some shooting yesterday.'

   b. ŋa məʃər ʃamndu ta-lɐn
    1SG yesterday gun UP+EVID:NFH-shoot
    'I did some shooting yesterday.'

For the present tense, if the subject is in first person, the prefix would be *ko-* (Lin does not mention whether this prefix has any evidential sense or not). If the subject is in non-first person, the prefix would be *na-* if the action is in short duration or is seen by the speaker, and it would be *ŋa-* if it lasts for a long period of time or is not witnessed (X. R. Lin 1993: 232). These are illustrated in (3) (X. R. Lin 1993: 232–3).

(3) a. ŋa ko-no-ŋ
    1SG PRS-drive-1SG
    'I'm driving (cattle).'

   b. no na-tə-no-u
    2SG PRS+EVID:FH-2-drive-2SG
    'You are driving (cattle).' (The speaker has visual evidence for the statement.)

   c. no ŋa-tə-no-u
    2SG PRS+EVID:NFH-2-drive-2SG
    'You are driving (cattle).' (The speaker does not have visual evidence for the statement.)

Cogtse thus has two firsthand versus non-firsthand evidential subsystems, which are marked in different patterns in different tenses. In the past tense situation, the marking pattern is privative, with the non-firsthand evidential formally marked and the firsthand evidential unmarked. In the present tense, the marking pattern is equipollent, with both firsthand and non-firsthand evidentials overtly coded in non-first person environments.

The primary meaning of the firsthand evidential in Cogtse is visual evidence [X. R. Lin (1993: 195) sometimes would just use 'witnessed' or 'non-witnessed' to capture the semantic contrast even in non-first person past situations], and meanings of familiarity and certainty can be seen as its extensions. [Although it should be noted that these senses can be hard to tease apart in many cases, as is shown in (1a)]. The non-volitional interpretation that arises from the co-occurrence of the first person with the non-firsthand evidential is the well-documented first-person effects.

2.1.2   Jiaomuzu Variety

The Jiaomuzu (a.k.a. Kyom-kyo) variety of Situ Rgyalrong, as reported in Prins (2011), has an evidential system that is similar to, yet in some ways more complex than, the Cogtse variety. The two varieties are similar in that both have a firsthand evidential and a non-firsthand evidential in the past tense. The Jiaomuzu variety in addition has a reported evidential and an observational evidential.[4]

Similar to Cogtse, Jiaomuzu also has a firsthand and a non-firsthand evidential distinction in the past tense [Prins (2011: 420) terms this distinction as 'direct' versus 'non-direct'], with only the non-firsthand evidential overtly marked. The firsthand evidential, with senses of 'eye-witness' or 'firsthand knowledge', is the default interpretation for a past tense clause unmarked for evidentiality (Prins 2011: 422). The meaning of the non-firsthand evidential is lack of firsthand knowledge, and if the subject is in first person, it implies that the speaker was unaware of their action or performed an action unwittingly (Prins 2011: 424).

While the encodings of non-firsthand information are superficially similar in Cogtse and Jiaomuzu, in that both vocalic change and stem alternation are involved, they are analyzed differently in the two varieties. Noticing that for clauses with the non-firsthand evidential, the vowels in the relevant affixes are unanimously *a* and the syllable in which the vowel appears always receives a

---

4   Prins (2011: 420) understands the conceptual basis of evidentiality in Jiaomuzu to be the speaker's conviction of how reliable his statement is. She therefore includes the copula verb *ŋos*, whose function is to denote the speaker's certainty of a situation, as a type of evidential (Prins 2011: 426). This form is excluded as it does not meet the definition of evidentiality adopted here. [Incidentally, Munya seems to have a cognate, *ŋo*, which functions as an equative copula and an egophoric marker. See Bai (2019: 246–8) for more discussion.] In spite of the fact that her characterization of evidentiality is different from what is defined in this study, most categories that she discusses have information source as their core meanings, they are thus treated as evidentials here.

heavy stress, Prins (2011: 423) posits a stressed *a-* morpheme for the non-direct evidential, which always merges with the preceding tense or aspect marker and is never pronounced alone. In addition, the non-firsthand evidential marked by *a-* needs to occur with verb root 1, while the firsthand evidential is only compatible with root 2 forms. Compare (4a), with a firsthand evidential, with (4b), which has a non-firsthand evidential (Prins 2011: 423).

(4) a. *pkraʃis w-əmpʰa-j   ji-rji*
       PN   3SG+GEN-outside-LOC PFV-go$_2$+EVID:FH
       'bKra-shis went out.'

  b. *pkraʃis malataŋ   kə-ndza   ji-'a-tʃʰi*
       PN   spicy.soup NOM-eat   PFV-EVID:NFH-go$_1$
       'bKra-shis went to have spicy soup.'

Prins (2011: 424) notices that a speaker's eye-witness perspective influences not just choice of evidentials but also person-number marking in Jiaomuzu. In particular, in a non-firsthand situation, the third person plural marking is preferred—even if the event may only include two participants—in order to signal that the speaker is not able to give precise detail. Consider the pair of examples below (Prins 2011: 424).

(5) a. *wuvjot   to-'a-ŋa-məcə-jn   kə-məŋkʰuʔ tʃe*
       much   PFV-EVID:NFH-REC-say-3PL   NOM-after   LOC
       to-'a-ŋa-le-leʔt-jn
       PFV-EVID:NFH-REC-REDU-hit$_1$-3PL
       'They talked back and forth and finally they started fighting.'

  b. *wuvjot   na-ŋa-məcə-**ndʒ**   kə-məŋkʰuʔ tʃe*
       much   PFV-REC-say+EVID:FH-3DU   NOM-after   LOC
       *to-ŋa-la-laʔt-**ndʒ***
       PFV-REC-REDU-hit$_2$+EVID:FH-3DU
       'They talked back and forth and finally they started fighting.'

The two examples describe the same event, which is an argument that deteriorates into a fight. In (5a), the use of the non-firsthand evidential indicates that the speaker did not witness the conflict in person. He may have acquired the information through hearsay and is aware that only two people were involved, but he nevertheless chooses the third person plural marker, in order to show generality or vagueness. (5b) suggests that the speaker saw the brawl and knew there were only two people involved, an information that is shown with the dual marker (Prins 2011: 424). (The verb root for 'say', *məcə*, has only one form and as a result does not show alternation.)

Jiaomuzu also has a reported evidential verb *ka-cəs* 'say' for information that is obtained from hearsay. This is illustrated in (6a) (Prins 2011: 428). It can be used in combination with the non-firsthand evidential to show the speaker's uncertainty of her statement, as in (6b) (Prins 2011: 427).

(6) a. *xolan   sok   ma-məʃtak   na-cəs*
    PN   manner   NEG-be.cold   PFV-say
    'Holland is not that cold, they said.'

b. *pkraʃis   kʰəna   na-'a-top-w   na-cəs-jn*
   PN   dog   PFV-EVID:NFH-hit-3SG   PFV-say-3PL
   'They said that bKra-shis hit the dog.'

Prins (2011: 428–38) also identifies an 'observational evidential' *'na-~'nə-* that can occur in both past and non-past situations.[5] Its function is to emphasize that the information is based on the speaker's personal experience, or observation of a fact, or personal involvement. It can be extended to denote the sense of mirativity, for an insider/outsider distinction, or to signal non-volitionality.

Prins (2011: 431–2) uses the following pair of examples to explicate the primary function of this evidential.

(7) a. *kom   kacu   ma-kʰut*
    door   open   NEG-possible
    'The door can't be opened.'

b. *kom   kacu   ma-'nə-kʰut*
   door   open   NEG-EVID:OBS-possible
   'I can't open the door.'

Prins explains that (7a), which is not formally marked for evidentiality, means that the speaker is certain that the door is impossible to open. He gains this knowledge through his own trial and is also positive that no one else will be able to open it. By contrast, (7b), with an observational evidential, means that

---

5 Prins (2011: 420–1) notes that this terminology is adopted from Y.-J. Lin (2000: 76–81), though the functions of it are in some ways different from the evidential described by Lin. While this marker seems to be formally related to the direct evidential *ɲɯ-* in Japhug (cf. §2.1.3), it is not analyzed as a direct evidential here as the functions and overtones of it are atypical of a direct evidential.

the speaker has tried to open the door but failed. He knows, from his own experience, that he himself cannot open the door, but there may be a person, somewhere, who is capable of opening it.

The mirative sense of this marker is shown with the pair of examples in (8) (Prins 2011: 433).

(8) a. ŋa   ŋ-əjeʔm   məntoʔk   ndoʔ
     1SG 1SG+GEN-house flowers   have
     'There are flowers in my house.'

b. ŋa   ŋ-əjeʔm   məntoʔk   **'na**-ndoʔ
    1SG 1SG+GEN-house flowers   EVID:OBS-have
    'There are flowers in my house!'

(8a) indicates that the speaker knows that there are flowers in his house for sure. (8b) means that the presence of flowers in the speaker's house is unexpected and comes as a surprise. They were not there before, and the speaker did not put them there, nor does he know how they came to be there (Prins 2011: 433).

The observational evidential also comes into play when 'a speaker wants to indicate his social position as an outsider or insider in relation to a group' (Prins 2011: 434). A person that belongs to the in-group (which is generally formed through kinship) is entitled to make statements conveying certainty, based on his status as an insider. In this case the observational evidential cannot be used. Whereas for a person who does not belong to the in-group, the observational evidential is required, regardless of his level of knowledge about a certain fact or situation (Prins 2011: 435). Consider the two examples below (Prins 2011: 434).

(9) a. jontan mə-ndoʔ
     PN   INTRG-have
     'Is Yon-tan home?'

b. jontan mə-**'na**-ndoʔ
    PN   INTRG-EVID:OBS-have
    'Is Yon-tan home?'

Only a person who is a family or kin of Yon-tan can say (9a), as he is an insider and is entitled to speak about Yon-tan with authority. (9b) is normally used by a person who is an outsider to the family, say a friend who comes looking for Yon-tan.

Another extended function of the observational evidential 'is to convey that there is third or outsider party involvement and control over an action or event'. This is illustrated in (10) (Prins 2011: 436).

(10) a. soʃnu pkraʃis wucɛn mi rjəʔk ra
    tomorrow PN 5000 meter run need
    'Tomorrow bKra-shis has to run the 5000m.'

 b. soʃnu pkraʃis wucɛn mi rjəʔk 'na-ra
    tomorrow PN 5000 meter run EVID:OBS-need
    'Tomorrow bKra-shis must run the 5000m.'

(10a) not only states that bKra-shis will perform the action of running the next day, it also shows the speaker's certainty that the event will take place. In example (10b), the presence of the observational evidential signals that some outside force compels bKra-shis to run, which maybe bKra-shis' coach in track and field or other factors. In any case, bKra-shis will run not out of his own will, but because of some external requirements (Prins 2011: 436).

2.1.3 Japhug Dialect

Evidentiality in Japhug Rgyalrong is briefly mentioned in Y.-J. Lin and Luo (2003), which deals with the Dazang variety, and more systematically explored in Jacques (2008, 2019), which mainly focus on the Kamnyu variety.

In Y.-J. Lin and Luo (2003), a study which focuses on the tense-aspect functions of directional prefixes and verb stem alternation in Dazang, an 'indirect perfect prefix' (*jianjie shizheng wanchengti qianzhui*) -*a* is recognized, which resembles the Jiaomuzu non-firsthand evidential marker in both form and function. Also similar to Jiaomuzu, in the Dazang variety, this marker always merges with its preceding prefix and is never independently realized. If the preceding prefix is a directional prefix, for which the vowels are either *u* or *ə*, to mark non-firsthand evidential, the vowel in that prefix needs to be changed to *o*. But if the prefix is the second person singular *tə-*, it would become *ta-*. With regard to its function, when this prefix appears in non-first person contexts, it denotes information that is not visually acquired or personally experienced by the speaker, but that is overheard or inferred or obtained from other non-firsthand sources. In first-person environments, the marker indicates that the action was carried out unconsciously by the speaker and is only realized afterwards. Other types of evidential are not mentioned in this study.

Evidentiality in Kamnyu, another variety of the Japhug dialect, is reported in Jacques (2008: 260–80, 2019). The two studies are largely complementary to each other, with the first one having a detailed discussion on the evidentials in the past tense while the second one specifically focusing on the system in the present tense. In general, evidentiality in the Kamnyu variety consists of a firsthand and a non-firsthand evidential in the past tense, a factual evidential and a direct evidential for stative verbs in the present tense, and a reported evidential.

Just like other dialects, there is a contrast between firsthand and non-firsthand evidentials in the past tense of this variety.[6] The firsthand sense is the default interpretation of a past tense clause and is not overtly marked, hence we only need to focus on the marking of the non-firsthand evidential.

Kamnyu is more complicated than other dialects in that marking of the non-firsthand evidential is influenced by the perfective versus imperfective distinction in the past tense. To signal the non-firsthand evidential in the past perfective situation, one needs to use the fourth set of directional prefixes,[7] and in the case of transitive verbs with a first or second person subject, the -t suffix needs to be added. To mark the non-firsthand evidential in the past imperfective, the only prefix that is allowed is *pɯ-/pjɤ-* 'downward'[8] (Jacques 2008: 261–3).

The semantics of non-firsthand evidential includes inference (11) and non-visual evidence. This evidential is also very commonly used for telling traditional stories (Jacques 2008: 272–3).

(11) kɯ-mɯrkɯ   nɯ   khɯɣɲɯ   ɯ-ŋgɯ
      NMLZ:SBJ-steal   DEM   window   3SG+POSS-inside
      lo-yi   ɲɯ-ŋu
      US+EVID:NFH-come   IMPF-be
      'The burglar climbed in through the window.' (Said by a police after seeing the footprints of the burglar.)

A stative verb with the perfective aspect indicates a change of state. If such a verb is marked for non-firsthand perfective evidential, it means that the

---

6 Jacques (2008: 260–1) labels this distinction as 'experiential' (*qinyan*) versus 'non-experiential' (*feiqinyan*), and notes that the non-experiential evidential corresponds to the indirect evidential in Dazang as mentioned above.

7 There are four sets of directional prefixes in Kamnyu, which differ from each other mostly in vowels and result from the merging of directional prefixes with different vocalic prefixes. The vowel in the fourth set is *-o* or *-ɤ*, which comes from merging with the vowels in the third set marker *-a/-ɤ* (Jacques 2008: 249).

8 The situation for the past imperfective becomes more complex if a verb stem has *a-* as its initial syllable. In this case, if the predicate is intransitive and the subject is in third person, the prefix *k-* needs to be inserted between the directional prefix and the verb stem. And for a transitive verb with third person arguments, the suffix *-chɯ* is additionally obligatorily added. For the analyses of these two affixes, see Jacques (2008: 262–3).

speaker only saw the result of the change, not the whole process, as in (12a). If the marker is non-firsthand imperfective, it means that the speaker is surprised by her new discovery, as in (12b) (Jacques 2008: 274–5).

(12) a. *tɯmgo ko-smi*
meal   PFV+EVID:NFH-be.cooked
'The meal is cooked ready.'

 b. *pjɤ-mpɕɤr   nɯ!*
    IMPF+EVID:NFH-be.beautiful   EXCLAM
    'How beautiful!' (The speaker just discovered this fact.)

When used with first person subjects, it means that the action is performed unconsciously, as in cases when the actor is drunk or has fallen ill (Jacques 2008: 275).

Jacques (2008: 272–3, 316, 2019) also briefly mentions a reported evidential, which is indicated with the sentence final particle *khi*. This marker is normally used in a sentence with the non-firsthand evidential, as in (13) (Jacques 2008: 273).

(13)   *tɕɤtu   zara   nɯ-ɴɢarmɯ   nɯ   pjɤ-si*
       above   3PL   3PL-mixed.cattle   DEM   PFV+EVID:NFH-die
       khi
       EVID:REP
       'It is said that the mixed cattle in the above village died.'

The fact that the reported evidential rarely occurs on its own may suggest that the reported evidential has not yet fully grammaticalized in Japhug.

Jacques (2019) identifies a tripartite evidential contrast for stative verbs in the present tense: factual, sensory and egophoric.[9] The egophoric 'is used to describe information that is not directly shareable, which the speaker obtains through his own personal involvement in a state of affairs'. Since this category does not fit into the present framework, it will not be discussed here.

The factual evidential 'expresses a fact regarded as true by the speaker or belonging to generally accepted knowledge'. It is expressed with bare verb stems alone, and can be seen as zero-marked, as in (14).

---

9 Due to the high complexity of the TAME morphology in Rgyalrong languages, Jacques only discusses the situation for stative verbs in this study. Hence the reader is reminded that what is presented below may not be totally applicable to dynamic verbs.

(14)   *aʑo   nɯra   fse-a*
           1SG   DEM+PL   be.like+EVID:FACTUAL-1SG
           tɕe   ŋgɯ-a
           LNK   be.poor+EVID:FACTUAL-1SG
           'I am poor like that.'

Since the semantic parameters covered by the sensory evidential is in many ways similar to that of a direct evidential, it is renamed as such in the following presentation for ease of comparison. This evidential is formed by combining the verb stem with the prefix *ɲɯ-* (the negative form is *mɯ́j-*).[10] It can occur with both past tense imperfective and present tense perfective. This evidential expresses information acquired through sense channels, which is mostly vision, but can also be hearing, touch, smell and taste. In (15), the evidence is tactile (Jacques 2019).

(15)   *ɲɯ́-wɣ-nɤmɤle   tɕe   ɲɯ-mpɯ*
           IMPF-INV-touch   LNK   EVID:DIRECT-be.soft
           'It is soft to the touch.'

This evidential can co-occur with endopathic verbs, such as those denoting pain, itch, cold, etc., as in (16) (Jacques 2019).

(16)   *tʰam   tɕe   mɯ́j-cʰa-a,   a-mi*
           now   LNK   EVID:DIRECT+NEG-can-1SG   1SG+POSS-foot
           ɲɯ-mŋɤm
           EVID:DIRECT-hurt
           'Now I can't, my foot hurts.'

It can also express surprise or imply the discovery of a previously unknown fact. For example, (17a) states a fact about the addressee that the speaker just noticed, and (17b) expresses the speaker's surprise (Jacques 2019).

(17)   a. *ɲɯ-tɯ-mkʰɤz*
              EVID:DIRECT-2-be.expert
              'You are good at it.'

---

10   Jacques (2008: 278) treats this prefix as an 'experiential' evidential (*qinyanshi*) and points out that it corresponds to the observational evidential identified in Y.-J. Lin (2000: 82) for the Cogtse variety.

b. *amaŋ,   nuusthuci   ɲɯ-mbro*
   EXCLAM   so.much   EVID:DIRECT-be.high
   'It is so high!'

Jacques (2019) therefore argues that the direct evidential in Japhug can have the mirative sense.

The direct evidential 'is also used concerning information that is somehow part of common knowledge, but that the speaker has not had the opportunity to personally confirm'. For instance, in (18), the speaker is describing facts about an animal that does not live in Tibetan areas, which he only knows indirectly (Jacques 2019).

(18)   *sɯŋgi   nɯ   ɲɯ-sɤɣ-mu*
       lion   DEM   EVID:DIRECT-DEEXP-be.afraid
       'The lion is terrifying.'

2.2   Khroskyabs

Based on shared innovations in phonology and morphology, Lai (2017: 11–5) identifies two major dialects of Khroskyabs, which are Core Khroskyabs and Njorogs, with the former containing several sub-dialects of four-levels. [A different classification can be found in B. F. Huang (2007: 155)].

Lai (2017) is the only work with a systematic discussion on evidentiality in Khroskyabs. His study mainly focuses on the Wobzi variety of Core Khroskyabs, but substantial references are also made to the Siyuewu variety. He identifies two evidentials in Wobzi: an inferential (inférentiel) evidential in the past tense, and a reported (ouï-dire) evidential. However, a close examination of his data and analyses reveals that if a clause in the past tense is not overtly marked for evidentiality, then the information is understood to be visually or perhaps directly acquired. Therefore, the system in Wobzi is reanalyzed as having a firsthand and non-firsthand evidential in the past tense, and also a reported evidential, with the firsthand evidential zero-marked and the non-firsthand evidential corresponding to the afore-mentioned inferential evidential.

The non-firsthand evidential is marked with the enclitic =*si*, which is mostly confined to the past tense and is rarely attested in non-past situations. This marker can be extended to express mirativity, and with first person subjects, it denotes speakers' in-volitionality or unawareness of their actions (Lai 2017: 495–500). Its evidential function is illustrated in (19) (Lai 2017: 495).

(19)   *dangao=tə   vluvzâŋ=ɣə   u-dzí=si*
       cake=DEF   PN=ERG   PST.INV-eat₁=EVID:NFH
       'Blobzang ate the cake.'

(Lai 2017: 495) explains that this sentence can be used if the speaker left a cake on the table before leaving her house but finds it gone on her return. She deduces that Blobzang ate the cake, because she saw him entering the house before her departure, which prompts the use of =*si*. He further remarks that, if this marker is not used, it would imply that the speaker saw Blobzang ate the cake. It is because of this that I argue that Wobzi has a zero-marked firsthand evidential.

(20) demonstrates the mirative sense of this marker (Lai 2017: 497).

(20) jdɜ̂=tə   pa   kə-rpʰɜ̂m=**si**
      river=DEF   all   PFV-freeze$_2$=EVID:NFH
      'The river is completely frozen!'

This sentence can be used if the speaker opens the window on a winter morning and finds that the river, which was still flowing yesterday, has frozen completely.

The first-person effects of this evidential can be seen from the pair of examples below (Lai 2017: 498).

(21) a. mbærkʰæ̂m   nə-ɕ-ôŋ
        PN   PST-go$_2$-1SG
        'I went to 'Barkhams.'

   b. mbærkʰæ̂m   nə-ɕ-ôŋ=**si**
        PN   PST-go$_2$-1SG=EVID:NFH
        'I went to 'Barkhams (without doing it on purpose).'

The first example is used in normal situations. The second example, with =*si* added, gives the impression that the speaker did not intend to go to 'Barkhams, and only realized it after getting there.

The reported evidential *rǽ* 'say' is used if the information is neither directly perceived nor inferred, but acquired through hearsay. While it is a verb that can take various prefixes, the agent, which denotes the original author of the information, is not overtly expressed, as in (22) (Lai 2017: 494).

(22) cɜ̂=yə   tsʰægí=tə   ɕsǽrpa   k-u-jdɔ́=ska   góŋ
      3SG=ERG   clothing=DEF   be.new   PST-INV-buy$_2$=NMLZ   price
      nœ-cʰî   r-u-rǽ
      IMPF.PST-be.great   NON.PST-INV-EVID:REP
      'It is said that this garment was expensive at the time of purchase.'

Different from the situation in Core Rgyalrong, directional prefixes in Wobzi have not acquired full-fledged evidential functions and can at best be treated as incipient evidential markers. Recall that in some Core Rgyalrong dialects, directional prefixes have developed evidential functions, and can mark the non-firsthand evidential via ablaut. In Wobzi, no such ablaut is documented, and the same directional prefix can code both firsthand [which Lai calls 'sensory' (sensoriel)] and non-firsthand [which Lai calls 'inferential' (inférentiel)] meanings (the interpretation depends on specific contexts), which are only found in the non-past tense. The firsthand 'concerns the sources of information directly conceived by the speaker, which can be visual, auditory, olfactory, kinesthetic or taste, etc.' (Lai 2017: 491), whereas the non-firsthand usage 'indicates that the source of information is not directly conceived by the speaker, and that the speaker is making inferences based on external evidence' (Lai 2017: 492).

Consider the two examples in (23) (Lai 2017: 491, 493).

(23) a. *cə ftɕalá=tə kâdə rə-lʁǽi ɕə*
   DEM thing=DEF too.much NONS-be.bulky$_1$ CONJ
   rə-scôcə-n rây̌may
   IMPF-move$_1$-2SG all.right
   'These things are too cumbersome, can you move them?'

b. *cə ʁjô=tə=gə kə-mbjæbjû-n tɕʰə gǎy tʰərə*
   DEM hole=DEF=LOC IMPF-peep$_1$-2 CONJ interior something
   rə-stî
   NONS-exist$_1$
   'Look in this hole, there is something (it seems to me).'

In both examples the prima facie evidential sense is conveyed through the erstwhile non-specific directional prefix *rə-*. In (23a), the speaker saw that things are blocking the way, so she asks the addressee to move them. The information here is obtained through a firsthand channel. In (23b), the speaker infers that there is something in the hole, which is presumably based on the noise coming out of it, or the unexpected reaction of an animal that has passed through it. The information in this case comes from non-firsthand source.

The fact that the same form expresses both firsthand sense and non-firsthand sense in the same environment is highly unusual. In view of this, Lai (2017: 504) concludes that 'in the non-past, evidentiality … is an extension of the use of directional prefixes, where the inferential and the sensory are morphologically ambiguous'. Directional prefixes in Wobzi Khroskyabs, therefore, has not grammaticalized into full-fledged evidentials.

2.3 Horpa

In a recent study, J. T.-S. Sun (2019a) proposes that Horpa can be divided into five languages: Central, Eastern, Northern, Western and Northwestern.[11] By far most studies, including all that will be mentioned in this section, are focused on the Central dialect. J. T.-S. Sun (2019a) points out that while Northern Horpa is more conservative and closer to Core Rgyalrong, Central Horpa is innovative in verbal morphology.

Tian (2019) briefly mentions that in Gexi, a variety of Central Horpa, there is an indirect evidential (*jianjie shizheng*) suffix -s^{h}i, which also has some mirative meanings. In another study based on the same variety, Tian and J. T.-S. Sun (2019) note that the past tense prefix *də-* has developed certain evidential senses, such as non-volitional (*wuxin*), accidental (*yiwai*) and inference based on observed results. In the following two sections, the evidential systems from another two varieties of the Central Dialect will be presented, which are Rtau and Geshiza.

2.3.1 Rtau Variety

In the Rtau variety, Jacques et al. (2017) document a sensory evidential *-rə* and an inferential evidential *-sə*. However, on closer examination, the evidential system seems to be one with a firsthand (which corresponds to the sensory evidential) and a non-firsthand (which corresponds to the inferential evidential) distinction in the past (or perfective) situation but simply a direct evidential in the non-past situation.

The direct evidential is only used in the non-past situation, and 'express[es] a … state or an action that the speaker is directly witnessing, be it by vision or by other senses.' (24) therefore can be uttered by someone who sees (or feels, in a car) the state of the road.

(24) tɕe ke rcɐ gə ŋə-rə
 road very be.bad INDEF be-EVID:DIRECT
 'It is a bad road.'

This evidential is not used in objective statement about the speaker himself, nor is it used with third person referents if the sentence conveys generally accepted knowledge. It can, however, be used to express endopathic sensations, knowledge or desire with the first person, as in (25).

---

11 A more preliminary, tripartite classification model is given in Jacques et al. (2017).

(25) ŋa   tɕa   tʰi-ʂpə   pre-rə
      1SG   tea   drink-want   want-EVID:DIRECT
      'I want to drink tea.'

The non-firsthand evidential marker 'indicates that the speaker learned of the facts in question second-hand (hearsay) or guessed them from indirect evidence',[12] as in (26).

(26) tsaɕi-w   dzɵma   de   nə-f-se-sə
      PN-ERG   PN   DEM   PFV-INV-kill-EVID:NFH
      'Bkrashis killed Sgrolma.'

For a perfective clause, if the suffix -sə is not present, it means that 'the speaker has firsthand authoritative knowledge of the events described.' Thus, uttered without -sə, (26) is only felicitous if the speaker witnessed the crime. In view of this, it can be said that in Rtau Horpa, there is a firsthand and non-firsthand contrast in past or perfective situations, with the firsthand evidential unmarked and the non-firsthand evidential shown with -sə.

2.3.2   Geshiza Variety

According to Honkasalo (2019: 581), evidentiality and the category of engagement[13] form one morphological paradigm in Geshiza, which are encoded with suffixes at slot 3 of the verbal template. Honkasalo (2019: 584) recognizes five evidential categories: Ego-oriented, sensory (renamed as 'direct' in the following presentation), inferential, reportative and quotative. The ego-oriented evidential is not overtly marked, and is often used with first-person participants. It pertains to 'direct personal experience and conscious participation' and can 'imply volitional action the speaker has control over and carries with intent' (Honkasalo 2019: 584–5). The major function of this category seems to be egophoric, therefore it is not treated as an evidential here. In the following discussion we will focus on the properties of the other four evidentials.

The direct evidential, marked with -ræ, expresses that the information source is sensory perception with one or more of the five sense organs. It

---

[12] This seems to imply that this marker is only used in perfective or past situations, although this issue is not explicitly mentioned by the authors.
[13] Following Evans, Bergqvist, and San Roque (2017), Honkasalo (2019: 581) defines this category as grammaticalized intersubjectivity that encodes 'relative accessibility of an entity or state of affairs to the speaker and addressee'.

can only be used in non-past tense situations. In (27), the information source coded is taste/smell (Honkasalo 2019: 587).

(27) tsʰə ɕ-no-ræ?
salt INTRG-smell/taste-EVID:DIRECT
'Is there enough salt in the food?'

When occurring with first person subjects, this evidential 'is used for states and actions that remain outside the subject's control and take place without explicit volition' (Honkasalo 2019: 603). Thus, it can be suffixed to verbs denoting endopathic processes, such as pain (28), and internal feelings with emotions (Honkasalo 2019: 588).

(28) lva ŋo-ræ
shoulder be.painful₃-EVID:DIRECT
'(My) shoulders are aching.'

The direct evidential cannot be used if a speaker judges herself having control over the sensations or mental processes, as in (29) (Honkasalo 2019: 604).

(29) ŋui=tʰə ŋa lmu=bɔ
past=DEM 1SG forget.1SG=MOD
'Let bygones be bygones. (lit. I will forget that past thing.)'

This evidential can sometimes signal that the source of information is generic knowledge, as in (30) (Honkasalo 2019: 588).

(30) rŋa və tɕʰa mbəzə vɕe-ræ
hunting do₃ when gunpowder need.NON.PST-EVID:DIRECT
'Gunpowder is needed when hunting.'

The inferential evidential -sʰi indicates that the source of information is based on inference from visible results and traces. It occurs exclusively with the past form of the verb. An example is given in (31) (Honkasalo 2019: 589).

(31) jovə=tɕe zdi dæ-v-kuɕ-sʰi
medial.river.side.LOC=INS wall PFV-INV-cut.PST.3-EVID:INFR
'It (the cow) broke a wall on the river side.' (The speaker sees the remains of a fence broken by the cow.)

This evidential also shows first-person effects. Honkasalo (2019: 604) points out that, 'when used with the first person, the inferential evidential indicates that the speaker did not carry out the action intentionally (i.e. inadvertent action), was unaware of it when it took place, or did not intend to cause the actual outcome,' as in (32) (Honkasalo 2019: 604).

(32) ŋa dæ-lmu-sʰi
1SG PFV-forget.1SG-EVID:INFR
'I forgot it.'

It can also be extended to denote mirativity, as in contexts where the speaker realizes something *post factum* (33a), or is surprised by new information (33b) (Honkasalo 2019: 606).

(33) a. məsni=tʰə sʰo tɕʰæræ mɛ-dəu-sʰi
today=TOP more thing ASP.NEG-do.1SG-EVID:INFR
'I did not do anything else today!'

b. ləspə rə-lxua-sʰi
body PFV-gain.weight.3-EVID:INFR
'You have gained weight!'

The reported evidential *-jə* signals that the information is overheard from other people, the source of which is unspecified. This is illustrated in (34) (Honkasalo 2019: 590).

(34) bəsni pʰjo-ræ-jə
today see.off.NON.PST-EVID:DIRECT-EVID:REP
'It is said that the seeing-off (i.e., funeral) is today.'

Honkasalo (2019: 591) remarks that this suffix originates from the verb *jə* 'to say', and the reported evidential results from a grammaticalized reported speech construction in which the originally independent speech-report verb has been reanalyzed as an evidential suffix.

In addition to the reported evidential, Geshiza also has a quotative evidential *-wo*, which allows the author of the reported information to be specified. This suffix most frequently attaches to the verb *jə* 'to say', as in (35), but other verbs of speaking, such as *amomo* 'to discuss', are also attested (Honkasalo 2019: 591–2).

(35) e=tʰə-tʰə   'bɔrqua   stʰə'   jə-wo
     DEM=TOP-REDU   throat   tighten.NON.PST.3   say.3-EVID:QUO
     '"My throat tightens (i.e., I am very angry)," he said.'

2.4 Qiang

Researchers generally agree that Qiang can be broadly divided into a northern dialect and a southern dialect (H. K. Sun 1981: 177–8), though there are disputes concerning the membership of certain varieties (Liu 1998: 16–8; LaPolla and C. L. Huang 2003: 2–3; B. F. Huang and Zhou 2006: 285–6).

Early grammar sketches of Qiang did not formally recognize any evidentiality system, only noting in passing certain grammatical morphemes that have some evidential flavor. For example, H. K. Sun (1981: 117) mentions that in Taoping Qiang, a southern dialect, the verbal suffix -ŋu indicates that the action is witnessed by the speaker, or even if it is not, the speaker has a high degree of certainty about the truth of the utterance. In a northern dialect, Mawo, the suffix -ni reported in Liu (1998: 177) has almost identical functions ('the action is witnessed by the speaker, and sometimes it shows that the speaker has a high degree of certainty towards the action').

The evidentiality systems of the currently reported Qiang dialects are similar to a large extent, generally consisting of a visual evidential, an inferential evidential, and a reported evidential. The visual evidential in certain varieties is optionally marked, and the inferential evidential can have mirative overtones and first-person effects.

We will next discuss in more details the evidentiality system in four varieties of Qiang: Ronghong (§2.4.1), Qugu (§2.4.2), Puxi (§2.4.3) and Longxi (§2.4.4). The first two varieties belong to the northern dialect and the rest are members of the southern dialect.

2.4.1 Ronghong Variety

Ronghong Qiang has a three-term evidential system: visual, inferential and reported, all marked via verbal suffixes (LaPolla 2003, see also LaPolla and C. L. Huang 2003: 197–211). The visual evidential marker -(w)u is used strictly for visual sensory information; the inferential evidential -k is applied when the information is derived from physical or other non-visual evidence; and the reported evidential -i is for reporting second-hand or third-hand knowledge of some situation or event that the speaker is unsure of. The visual and inferential evidential can be used for past or ongoing events, but not future events, and the reported evidential can be used for future or presently ongoing events or relatively recent past events (LaPolla 2003).

It is worth noting that in Ronghong Qiang, the visual evidential marker is often not obligatory for witnessed events—an unmarked clause is often assumed to represent information acquired first-hand or through seeing. The marker is used when the actor is animate and for emphasizing that the speaker really saw the action of other person(s) (LaPolla 2003). Consider (36a), which has a visual evidential marker, and (36b), which is not overtly marked for evidentiality but still implies that the information is visually acquired (LaPolla 2003).

(36) a. *the: zdʑyta: ɦa-qə-(w)u*
    3SG PN+LOC DOWN-go-EVID:VIS
    'He went to Chengdu.' (used in a situation where the speaker saw the person leave and that person has not yet returned.)

 b. *ʔũ tɕeχun tu-pu-ji-n*
    2SG marry UP-do-CSM-2SG
    'You got married.' (I saw you get married.)

When used with the first person actor, the visual evidential suffix denotes unintentional or inadvertent action (LaPolla 2003). This is shown in (37) below.

(37) *qa the: ta de-we-ʐ-u-a*
    1SG 3SG LOC TS-have/exist-CAUS-EVID:VIS-1SG
    'I hit him (accidentally).' (The context for this was the speaker having hit the person while leaning back and stretching his arms back without looking behind him.)

This extension of the visual evidential seems to be unusual, as normally the overtones that such a category has is that the speaker vouches for the reliability of the information, or is certain about it (Aikhenvald 2004: 189).

The inferential evidential marker *-k* has a mirative extension. When the action involved is an activity, as in (38a), the suffix denotes the primary, inferential sense; when it is a state or the resulting state of some action, the meaning is mirativity (38b) (LaPolla 2003).

(38) a. *the: zdʑyta: ɦa-qə-k*
    3SG PN+LOC DOWN-go-EVID:INFR
    'He went to Chengdu.' (Used in a situation where the speaker knew the person was supposed to go to Chengdu, but wasn't sure when,

and then saw the person's luggage gone, so assumed he had left for Chengdu. /-k/ could not be used if the speaker saw the person leave.)

    b. *dzy*   *de-zge-ji-k!*
       door   TS-open-CSM-EVID:INFR
       'The door is open!' (just discovered; see that the door is open, but don't know who opened it.)

Used with first person actors, the inferential evidential marker not only means that the action was just discovered, but also that it was unintentional or originally unknown, as is shown in (39) (LaPolla 2003).

(39)   (*qa*)   *dzy*   *ɦa-mə-sua-k-a!*
      1SG   door   DOWN-NEG-lock-EVID:INFR-1SG
      'I didn't lock the door!' (Used in a situation where the speaker had thought he had locked the door.)

The visual evidential and the inferential evidential can be used together, for a situation where the speaker makes a supposition which later on gets confirmed. For example, if the speaker guessed that someone was playing drums next door, then went there and found the person holding a drum or drumsticks, then he can say (40).

(40)   oh   *the:*   *z̪bə*   *z̪ete-k-u!*
      oh   3SG   drum   play-EVID:INFR-EVID:VIS
      'Oh, he WAS playing a drum!'

The reported evidential *-i*, which is grammaticalized from the verb *jə~ji* 'to say', is used for hearsay, as in (41).

(41)   *the:*   *zdzyta:*   *ɦa-qə-i*
      3SG   PN+LOC   DOWN-go-EVID:REP
      'He went to Chengdu (I heard).'

If this suffix is used in a clause with the first person singular marking on the verb, as in (42), then it should be interpreted similarly to a direct quote, in spite of the fact that the actor is in third person.

(42)   *the:*   *ɕtɕimi*   *zdza-i*
      3SG   heart   sick+1SG-EVID:REP
      'He is unhappy. (He told me.)'

In this example it is the actor (the referent of 'he') who told the speaker that he himself is unhappy. If the person marking is the third person form, then the interpretation would be that someone other than the actor told the speaker that the actor was unhappy.

The reported evidential can be used together with the inferential evidential for accounting distant past events. The function here is to show a greater degree of uncertainty, which is often found in traditional stories, as in (43).

(43)   qeː-qeː-tu   ɦala   kapətʂ   kou
         before-before-LNK   INTERJ   orphan   INDEF+one+CL
         ŋuə-k-əi-tɕu
         COP-EVID:INFR-EVID:REP-SFP
         '(It is said) in the past there was an orphan.'

2.4.2   Qugu Variety

In their grammar of Qugu Qiang, B. F. Huang and Zhou (2006: 152–7) view evidentiality as a kind of modality category (*qingtai fanchou*), which additionally includes what in the present analysis can be seen as non-volitionality ['speaker's evaluation on actors' state of consciousness in the course of their action (for example, whether it is carried out voluntarily or involuntarily, or in self-control or out-of-control)'] and mirativity ['speaker's perception ... of other people's action (such as whether it is expected or unexpected)'] (B. F. Huang and Zhou 2006: 152). They clearly recognize evidentiality in this dialect and describe it as 'speakers' way of perceiving other people's action (such as whether the speaker has witnessed the whole process or is inferring from visible results, or whether it is through hearsay, or prediction, or assumption)' (B. F. Huang and Zhou 2006: 152). They specifically point out that by 'way of perceiving' they mean 'ways of acquiring information', and admit that it corresponds to what is referred to as evidentiality (B. F. Huang and Zhou 2006: 152, footnote 1).

While their insightful treatment reflects the fact that in Qugu Qiang these categories are interrelated, from a typological perspective this 'modality category' can be analyzed as primarily evidential in nature, with the non-volitional and mirative senses being semantic extensions of the inferential evidential (the three senses are all expressed with the -*k* suffix), which is how the system will be presented here.

There are five evidentials in Qugu Qiang, which are visual, inferential, reported, predictive and assumed. They are generally marked with one or two verbal suffixes, and some categories require that the verb take certain aspect, which is also shown through affixation.

The visual evidential [which they term as 'eye-witnessing modality' (*qinjian qingtai*)] -*w* is used when the speaker has witnessed the whole process of the action carried out by a third-person participant, as in (44) (B. F. Huang and Zhou 2006: 155).

(44) χumtɕi ʐetqupu ʔeze ɦɕe-qə̝te-w
      PN   hare   one   PFV-kill-EVID:VIS
      'χumtɕi killed a hare.'

The inferential evidential [which they call 'indirectly-knowing modality' (*jian-zhi qingtai*)] is used if 'the speaker did not witness the process of the action carried out by a third-person participant, but infers from the results of action or other indirect evidence that the participant either has done something, or did something recently, or that something has happened' (B. F. Huang and Zhou 2006: 154). This is marked by adding the suffix -*k* after the perfective form (indicated with a directional prefix), or after the immediate perfective form (marked with a directional prefix plus the immediate aspect marker -*jy*[14]) of the verb (B. F. Huang and Zhou 2006: 154). Some examples are given in (45).

(45) a. *qupu kə-jy-k   wa:!*
        3SG   go-IMM-EVID:INFR EXCL
        'He has left! (Uttered after seeing, for example, that the door to his house is locked, or that the bike that he often rides is gone.)'

   b. *nəj   mæχa   mujy de-ɬie-k   wa!*
      yesterday night rain PFV-fall-EVID:INFR EXCL
      'It rained last night! (Uttered after seeing that the ground is all wet.)'

   c. *tsa   mə   gəʴ   petɕin mə
      here weather be.cloudy   PN   weather
      tə-ʂqa-k*
      PFV-be.clear-EVID:INFR
      'The weather is cloudy here, but clear in Beijing.' (The speaker got this information from radio or TV.)

Example (45c) shows that in Qugu Qiang, people tend to use the inferential evidential for information acquired through new practices (cf. Aikhenvald 2014).

---

14   B. F. Huang and Zhou (2006: 145) call this suffix *qingti*, where *qing* can mean either 'modality' (*qingtai*) or 'situation' (*qingkuang*) (or something else), and *ti* means 'aspect'. They explain that this form 'signals that the action takes place near to the time of speech, or the emergence of new situations, or expecting that the situation would change'. For want of a suitable terminology, here I translate it as 'immediate aspect' and gloss it as -IMM.

The inferential evidential can also be used to report 'certain actions carried out by an actor while he is in an unmindful state, with no will of himself, or unconsciously' (B. F. Huang and Zhou 2006: 152). [They analyze this as an independent function, which they refer to as 'unconscious modality' (*buzijue qingtai*).] In this case, -*k* should be suffixed to the verb root and before aspect or person suffixes, if there is any (B. F. Huang and Zhou 2006: 152). Two examples are given below.

(46) a. qa   pəs   ti-ʑdʑi-æ   ɕi   dzə   bəl
       1SG today   PFV-be.ill-1SG   because   work   do
       do-mu-jy-**k**-a
       TS-NEG-finish-EVID:INFR-1SG
       'Because I went ill today, I didn't finish my work.' (The speaker didn't leave the work unfinished intentionally.)

   b. qupu   tə-waɬ-**k**-jy   ɕi   doqu   te: ti-de
      3SG   UP-big-EVID:INFR-IMM   because   pants   DEF   PFV-wear
      mo-gu-jy
      NEG-fit-IMM
      'He has grown up (unknowingly) and can no longer wear this pair of pants.'

Note that in (46a) the participant is in first person and in (46b) it is in third person. B. F. Huang and Zhou (2006: 152) point out that when this marker is used for unconscious action, the actor can be in any person, and the verb can be volitional or non-volitional. This indicates that -*k* is not used for first-person effects here, as the senses of non-volitionality or unconsciousness are not restricted to the first-person context. The inferential evidential in Qugu seems to have a more general overtone of simply denoting non-volitionality.

Another semantic extension of the inferential evidential is to express mirativity, which is used when 'the speaker is surprised by other people's action or behavior'. B. F. Huang and Zhou (2006: 153) treat this as an independent function, which they call 'surprise modality' (*yiwai qingtai*). In this case -*k* also immediately follows the verb root. The participant is in third person in (47a) and second person in (47b) (B. F. Huang and Zhou 2006: 153).

(47) a. tsʰua   baɬ   tse: tə-bəl   do-jy-**k**   wa!
       bridge   big   this   PFV-make   TS-finish-EVID:INFR   EXCL
       'This big bridge has already been built!'

b. *ʔu qəəˈ jæn ma-tsʰe-n, pəs̪*
   2SG before cigarette NEG-smoke-2SG now
   tsʰe-k-jy-n-a:?
   smoke-EVID:INFR-IMM-2SG-INTRG
   'You didn't smoke before, but you smoke now?'

The reported evidential [which they call 'hearsay modality' (*tingshuo qingtai*)] signals that the information is acquired through hearsay (B. F. Huang and Zhou 2006: 155). This is marked by the suffix *-ji*, as in (48).

(48)   *ʔili tsɯse bəl-a:-j-ji*
     2PL marriage do-FUT-2PL-EVID:REP
     'It is said that you two are getting married.'

According to B. F. Huang and Zhou (2006: 155), the reported evidential developed from the speech report verb *ji* 'say'. They deduce that *-ji* was reanalyzed as an evidential marker probably after the generic subject that refers to the author of the reported speech was omitted from the speech report construction.

There are two differences between the reported evidential *-ji* and the speech report verb *ji*. Firstly, the speech report verb can take a person-number suffix, which is impossible for the reported evidential. Secondly, in a speech report construction, the verb in the complement clause always takes a first-person suffix, while for the verb that takes the evidential marker, the person-number suffix is determined by the subject (B. F. Huang and Zhou 2006: 156). These are illustrated in (49), where the first example contains a reported evidential and the second a speech report verb (B. F. Huang and Zhou 2006: 155–6).

(49) a. *ʔu stuaχa sə-tʰə-jy-n-ji*
      2SG meal PFV-eat-IMM-2SG-EVID:REP
      'It is said that you already had your meal.'

   b. *ʔu sə-tʰə-jy-æ ji-n tɕʰi, qa stuaχa*
      2SG PFV-eat-IMM-1SG say-2SG because 1SG meal
      tə-mə-bəl-a
      PFV-NEG-make-1SG
      'Since you said "I have had my meal", I didn't cook.'

The predictive evidential [which they call 'predictive modality' (*yuce qingtai*)] reflects 'speakers' prediction of what will happen to other person or the outside world based on the surrounding environment or general knowledge' (B. F. Huang and Zhou 2006: 156). It is marked by suffixing *-ji* to the prospective aspect form of non-volitional verbs, and then adding the immediate aspect suffix -jy. The prospective aspect in Qugu is formed by suffixing -a: or -æ: to the verb root or changing the major vowel in the verb root to /a:/ or /æ:/. Two examples are given below (B. F. Huang and Zhou 2006: 156).

(50) a. *mujy* **ɬiæ:-ji-jy**
   rain fall+FUT-EVID:PRE-IMM
   'It will rain.'

   b. *ʔili guəs ʔə-ʂtʂa-ʂu-j,* ***lianthaː-ji-jy***
   2PL clothes IN-be.little-over-2PL catch.cold+FUT-EVID:PRE-IMM
   'You wear too little clothes, you will catch a cold.'

B. F. Huang and Zhou (2006: 156) point out that the predictive evidential cannot be used with first person, but they did not mention whether or not it can only be used with non-volitional verbs.

The assumed evidential [which they call 'the assumptive modality' (*tuice qingtai*)] is used 'when the speaker, based on what is known to her, makes assumptions about what other people will do or have done' (B. F. Huang and Zhou 2006: 156). This is indicated by adding the suffix *-tɕi* to the end of the verb stem and inserting *-a:* or *-æ:* between the verb root or aspect suffix and the person suffix.

The assumed evidential differs from the predictive evidential in two ways. Firstly, the assumed evidential can be used with first person, which is impossible for the predictive evidential. Secondly, the assumed evidential can be used for both past and future actions, while the predictive evidential can only be used for future situations (B. F. Huang and Zhou 2006: 156–7). Consider the three examples in (51) (B. F. Huang and Zhou 2006: 157).

(51) a. *qupu ləyʐ.susta* ***ka:-tɕi***
   3SG school go+EVID:ASU-EVID:ASU
   'He will probably go to school.'

   b. *ʔu stuaχa* ***sə-tʰə-jy-æː-n-tɕi***
   2SG meal PFV-eat-IMM-EVID:ASU-2SG-EVID:ASU
   'You probably have had your meal.'

   c. *qa tɕila kə la* ***ka:-tɕi***
   1SG where go also go+EVID:ASU-EVID:ASU
   'Wherever I want to go, it is possible for me to go there.'

Note that the suffix -*a:* or -*œ:* is fused with the verb root *kə* 'go' in (51a) and (51c) but is realized as an independent morpheme in (51b). It is used in a third person future situation in (51a), second person past situation in (51b), and first person future situation in (51c). B. F. Huang and Zhou (2006: 156) point out that when used with the first person, the assumed evidential has overtones of retort or challenge. For example, (51c) can mean 'I can go wherever I want to go, and it is not your business.'

2.4.3   Puxi Variety

According to C. L. Huang (2004: 195–7), there are three evidentials in Puxi Qiang, which are the formally unmarked visual evidential, the inferential evidential and the reported evidential.

The visual evidential is termed 'direct evidential' in C. L. Huang (2004: 195). However, his description of this category, which says '[t]he unmarked clause expresses knowledge which the speaker has from having seen the situation' (C. L. Huang 2004: 195–6), indicates that it may be more appropriate to call it a visual evidential. As has been noted above, a clause not formally marked for evidentiality has a visual evidential interpretation, as in (52) (C. L. Huang 2004: 196).

(52)   tʰala   zdʑeta   ʂe-ke-i
        3SG   PN   DS-go-CSM:3
        'S/he went to Chengdu.'

The inferential evidential -*ba* is marked clause-finally, and 'denotes evidence that the speaker obtained based on seeing the result of the action' (C. L. Huang 2004: 196), as in (53) (C. L. Huang 2004: 197).

(53)   tʂuʐoŋtɕi   tsoŋli   χqan   kue-lu-i-*ba*
        PN   premier   PN   IN-come-CSM:3-EVID:INFR
        '(I guess) Premier Zhu came to Mao County.'

The reported evidential -*u* (which is grammaticalized from *u* 'say') is suffixed to the end of the verb complex, indicating that the speaker is reporting a second-hand information, as is illustrated with (54) (C. L. Huang 2004: 196).

(54)   tʰala   zdʑeta   ʂe-ke-i-*u*
        3SG   PN   DS-go-CSM:3-EVID:REP
        '(I heard) s/he went to Chengdu.'

2.4.4 Longxi Variety

Zheng (2016: 384–95) reports five evidentials in Longxi Qiang: visual, inferential, hearsay, mirative and egophoric/heterophoric. The last two do not fit into the definition of evidential in this study, hence in the following discussion we will only consider the visual evidential, the inferential evidential, and the reported evidential.

The visual evidential signals that the information is obtained visually. Similar to Ronghong Qiang, formal marking of the visual evidential is optional. To overtly indicate this information source, one needs to use the enclitic =tɕʰi (Zheng 2016: 384). (55) is uttered when the speaker saw his wife (Zheng 2016: 384).

(55)   tʰò   jì=**tɕʰi**.   qà   zo   lân
      there   COP=EVID:VIS   1SG   wait   ATT
      '(My wife) is there. (She) is waiting for me.'

The visual evidential can be extended to mean that what is stated is obviously true. In (56), this sense is reinforced by *tánzàn* 'of course' (Zheng 2016: 386).

(56)   mí-kuà-tà=la   joŭ   **tánzàn**   miá-qà=**tɕʰi**
      NEG-handle-V=NON.FIN   still   of.course   NEG:CON-can=EVID:VIS
      'Of course, not handling (children's things) is still not practical.'

Visual evidentials with epistemic extensions of certainty are found in many languages, see Aikhenvald (2004: 170–1) and Aikhenvald (2018) for more discussion.

The inferential evidential marker =*wù* 'indicates that conclusions are inferred from available information' (Zheng 2016: 386). An example is given in (57) (Zheng 2016: 387).

(57)   veř   àpà   tʰe   ánə=χe   bó=χè   tɕìpi   à-wo   ŋu
      2SG: may   there   where=LOC   high=LOC   child   one-CL   COP
      pù=ɕi=**wù**
      do=2PL:PFV=EVID:INFR
      'You may (find) a child on high (hill).' (The speaker saw a child who she did [not] know before, so she inferred that this child was from the high hill.)

The reported evidential =ǰʅ marks information obtained from hearsay, and can have overtones of uncertainty (Zheng 2016: 389). An example is given in (58) (Zheng 2016: 389).

(58) ɳàpʰa kà-tɕè   lià=ʒ́ˡ   wè. ɳìtsə́=zu
    man INDEF-CLF:MAN COP=EVID:REP ATT night=TOP
    dà-wa kə̀=pù=ʒ́ˡ   wè
    CS-call go=HET=EVID:REP ATT
    '(I heard) there was such a man. (I heard) he went to call (Yu Chengfa) at night.'

The reported evidential can be used in combination with the inferential evidential. This can express a higher degree of uncertainty compared to using the reported evidential alone (Zheng 2016: 389), as in (59) (Zheng 2016: 390).

(59) tʰí-nə́ɕì-tì   χeí=wú=ʒ́ˡ   wè
    that-yesterday-that good=EVID:INFR=EVID:REP ATT
    '(I heard) (the song sung) yesterday is good.'

While this usage is similar to that in Ronghong Qiang (§2.4.1), the difference between the two dialects is that in Ronghong Qiang this double marking of evidentiality can only denote distant past events, but in Longxi Qiang it can refer to events that happened recently (Zheng 2016: 389–90), which can be seen from (59) above.

The reported evidential is historically derived from the speech report verb ʒ́ˡ 'say'. Although identical in form, only the speech report verb can take person marking, or be followed by clause final particles, or express the author of the reported speech as the actor of the speech report construction (Zheng 2016: 390–1).

2.5 nDrapa

As a smallish Qiangic language, nDrapa has two mutually intelligible dialects, which are the Upper nDrapa and the Lower nDrapa (B. F. Huang 1990; Gong 2007: 11). Both dialects have a direct evidential and an inferential evidential. However, the direct evidential is unmarked in the Upper dialect but indicated with the perfective marker ʂtɹ³³ in the Lower dialect. There is a reported evidential in the Upper dialect but three in the Lower dialect, and the Lower dialect in addition has a quotative evidential.

2.5.1   Upper Dialect

Evidentiality in the Upper dialect is briefly touched upon in B. F. Huang (1990) and Gong (2007: 84–5), and more thoroughly discussed in Shirai (2007). We will first look at how it is treated in the first two studies, before turning to the third one.

B. F. Huang (1990) mentions that there are four mood suffixes in Upper nDrapa that are used to describe the completed actions of third person actors. They code different degrees of certainty caused by different means of perception. The experiential mood (*qinyan yuqi*) *-ki³³* is used if the speaker saw the whole process of an action, the inferential mood (*panduan yuqi*) *-kia³³* is chosen if the speaker only saw the result of an action, the hearsay mood (*wenzhi yuqi*) *-tia³³* is for information acquired through hearsay, and the assumed mood (*cezhi yuqi*) *-a³³* is employed if the statement is based on deduction or other indirect means, and is typically used with non-volitional verbs. From the present perspective, the functions of these suffixes can be viewed as primarily evidential. However, she does not mention the situation for non-completed actions.

Gong (2007: 84–5) recognizes an experiential (*qinyan*) and a non-experiential (*feiqinyan*) mood in third person perfective contexts. The experiential mood is used if the speaker personally experienced an event, while the non-experiential mood is for information acquired through inference, assumption or other indirect ways. The experiential mood is not overtly marked, and the non-experiential mood is marked via the clause-final particle a^{31}. This resembles the firsthand and non-firsthand distinction that is commonly found in Rgyalrongic languages. This contrast is illustrated in (60) (Gong 2007: 85).

(60) a. $tʊ^{31}zə^{55}$ $kə^{55}$-$tsʅ^{55}$ $ʂtʅ^{55}$
   3SG   US-eat   PFV
   'He has eaten.'

   b. $tʊ^{31}zə^{55}$ $kə^{55}$-$tsʅ^{55}$ $ʂtʅ^{55}$ a^{31}
   3SG   US-eat   PFV   NON.EXPR
   'He has eaten.'

Shirai (2007) identifies three evidentials in the Mätro variety, which are the formally unmarked direct evidential, the inferential evidential *ba* and the reported evidential *dɛ*.

The zero-marked direct evidential is illustrated with (61), which was uttered as the speaker directly observed the rain falling outside the window.

(61)   ʼmoʔgu   ʼa-dɛ=ɖ-ɛ
      rain   DOWN-fall=IMPF-DISJ
      'It's raining.'

The inferential evidential indicates that 'the speaker has not directly witnessed the event and is not fully confident about the propositional content.' The inference can be based on visual or non-visual evidence, or general assumptions. An example is given in (62).

(62) ˉŋoro ˊjo-rɛ=ɴtsa ˉɴtsɛɖose ˉdo-tɕo=**ba**
 3SG friend-PL=with dance NONS-come/go=EVID:INFR
 'I guess she went dancing with friends (because she seemed happy before she went out).'

The reported evidential is used if the speaker acquired the information from other people, as in (63).

(63) ˊmoʔgu ˊa-dɛ ˊɖ-ɛ=**dɛ**
 rain DOWN-fall IMPF-DISJ=EVID:REP
 'I heard that it's raining.'

nDrapa is peculiar in that if the reported information is about the original speaker, the logophoric pronoun ˊtʉ needs to be used, as in (64).

(64) ˊjɛnʌ ˊ**tʉ** ˊzjɛ ˉgə-dzɛ ˊʜɟi=**dɛ**
 yesterday LOG antiphonal.song US-sing PST.1=EVID:REP
 '(According to him$_i$,) yesterday he$_i$ sang antiphonal songs.'

Contrary to B. F. Huang (1990) and Gong (2007: 84–5), Shirai (2007) rejects the analysis of *a* (which she treats as a suffix) as an evidential marker, even though she admits that it has certain evidential connotations. She notes that, in contrast to clauses unmarked by -*a*, a clause containing this suffix indicates a speaker's non-participation in the event, or that he only observed the event or its result. Compare the pair of sentences below.

(65) a. ˉŋoro ˉʌ-ʜsɨ-***a***
 3SG UP-recover-DISJ
 'She has recovered.'

 b. ˉŋoro ˉʌ-ʜsɨ
 3SG UP-recover
 'She (the one to whom I attended) has recovered.'

She explains that (65a) refers only to the resultant status, while (65b) implies that the speaker has been tending to a sick person and is directly aware of the process of the person's recovery.

In addition, she points out that this marker generally occurs in non-first person environments, is not allowed in a speech report if the subject of the matrix clause is co-referential with that of the embedded clause, and can be used in clauses with non-volitional predicates (regardless of the person of the subject). In view of these, she argues that this reflects the existence of the conjunct/disjunct distinction in nDrapa and that -*a* should be analyzed as a disjunct marker. This approach seems to be endorsed by Y. Huang (2019a), who views this distinction as one of egophoric versus non-egophoric, with the non-egophoric function marked by -*a* and the egophoric function unmarked.

2.5.2 Lower Dialect

Y. Huang (2019b) identifies six evidentials in Lower nDrapa, which are visual, non-visual sensory, inferential, reported, quotative, and factual. The visual evidential and the non-visual sensory evidential are marked with the same morpheme, *ʂtɪ^{33}*, which also denotes the perfective aspect. [This is treated as a perfective marker in Gong (2007: 84–5), which can be seen from (60).] According to Y. Huang (2019b), the visual evidential indicates information acquired through eye-witness while the non-visual sensory evidential denotes information obtained via non-visual sensory channels. In view of this, the visual evidential function and the non-visual sensory evidential function of *ʂtɪ^{33}* can be coalesced into one, i.e. as a direct evidential. Also, since the factual evidential pertains to 'certainty about the truthfulness of the information and the reliability of the proposition', it is not treated as an evidential in this study. Therefore, in what follows four evidentials will be discussed, which are the direct evidential, the inferential evidential, the reported evidential, and the quotative evidential.

(66) illustrates the use of the direct evidential.

(66) a. ŋue^{33}vʐʅ^{53} se^{33}pə^{55}ta^{33} tɛ^{55}-tɕy^{55} kə^{55}-^{h}tsʅ^{55}-ʂtɪ^{33}
       bear   hare   one-CLF   US-eat-EVID:DIRECT
    'The bear ate a hare.' (I saw that.)

b. tse^{55}me^{55} a^{55}-ʂtɕa^{55}-mbə^{33}rə^{33} me^{55} mui^{33}mui^{33} tɪ^{33}
   just.now   DOWN-boil-REL   medicine   very   one+CLF
   ʂkɪ^{55}-ʂtɪ^{53}
   be.bitter-EVID:DIRECT
   'The medicine that was boiled just now tastes very bitter.'

The inferential evidential *-mba* indicates that the statement is made based on inference or assumption, as in (67).

(67) mo⁵⁵gu⁵⁵ nɛ⁵⁵nə³³ a⁵⁵-ʰti⁵³ ʃʰo⁵⁵nə⁵⁵ a⁵⁵-ʰtɛ⁵⁵
rain two.days DOWN-fall.PFV tomorrow DOWN-fall
ma⁵⁵-ndu³³-**mba³³**
NEG-MOD-EVID:INFR
'It has been raining for two days, (I assume) it wouldn't rain tomorrow.'

There are three reported evidentials in Lower nDrapa, which are *-dɛ³³/-dɛ³³-dzɛ³³*, *-dɛ³³dzɛ³³* and *-dzɛ³³dɛ³³*. They originate from verbs of speech or their combinations.

-dɛ³³/-dɛ³³dzɛ³³ is a generic reported evidential, which is used for hearsay with unspecific sources, as in (68).

(68) ʔo²⁴ ʂtʂo⁵⁵-zə⁵⁵ nbe³³lɿ⁵⁵ tʂɿ³³ a⁵⁵-tʰo³³-ʂtia³³-**dɛ³³**
INTERJ life-FOC all skin DOWN-skin-PFV-EVID:REP
'Oh, it is said that all that were alive were skinned.'

-dɛ³³dzɛ³³ is normally found in story-telling:

(69) tə³³ta⁵³ ɕi⁵⁵ɕi⁵⁵ bdze³³-a⁵⁵-zɿ³³-**dɛ³³dzɛ³³**
DEM always say.PFV-NON.EGO-FACT-EVID:REP
'(According to stories,) it is always like that.'

-dzɛ³³dɛ³³ is used to report third-hand information:

(70) ɬa³³mu⁵³ ʃʰo³³nə⁵³ ɕʰa²⁴-tsə³³-**dzɛ³³dɛ³³**
PN tomorrow leave-PROS-EVID:REP
'It is said that Lhamu is leaving tomorrow.'

-dɛ³³ can also act as a quotative evidential, in which case it is marked after the quoted speech, as in (71).

(71) tɯ³³zə⁵³-wu³³ "ma³³-ɕʰu⁵⁵"-**dɛ³³** bdze³³-a⁵⁵-zɿ³³
3SG-DAT NEG-need-EVID:QUO say-NON.EGO-FACT
'(The daughter made up her mind and) said to him, "there is no need" (to be with him anymore).'

2.6 Munya

Munya is traditionally believed to have an eastern dialect and a western dialect, which are separated by the Mount Gongga (e.g. H. K. Sun 1983; B. F. Huang 1985). Till now, the bulk of research on this language is focused on the western dialect, with the eastern dialect virtually un-described. Recent studies have shown that the western dialect can be further divided into a northern and a southern dialect (Bai 2021), and they do not seem to have any significant difference in evidentiality. The system to be presented below is mainly based on Bai (2019), which draws on data from the northern dialect.

There are three evidentials in Munya—a direct evidential *ra*, an inferential evidential *sə*, which also functions as a perfect aspect marker, and a reported evidential *tə́pi*. The first two are auxiliary verbs and can take an interrogative or a negative prefix, while the reported evidential is a clause final particle and does not show any morphological change.

The direct evidential marker *ra* cannot be used for future situations. When used after a dynamic verb, it denotes an accomplished event, and when used after a stative verb, it signals an on-going or past state (the interpretation depends on the context). While this evidential is most commonly used to indicate that the information is visually acquired (72a) (native speakers often say 'you use it because you saw such and such happened'), the source can also be auditory (72b), olfactory (72c), or simply personal experience (72d) (Bai 2019: 235–6).

(72) a. tó-zə   tʰó-tso   ra
       one-CLF:MAN TS-run   EVID:DIRECT
       'A (person) ran away.'

   b. ndɛ   á-ra?
      sense.2SG INTRG-EVID:DIRECT
      'Did you sense (hear) (it)?'

   c. ɲí   ti   tó-lö   tə-né   ti
      1SG+ERG   something   one-CLF:GENR   UP-stink   STA
      ndá   ra
      sense.1SG EVID:DIRECT
      'I can sense (smell) that something stinks.'

   d. tɕə́tɕə   tʰə-vá   ra
      long.time TS-become   EVID:DIRECT
      '(It) has been a long time.'

There are interesting interactions between this evidential marker, person of subject, and volitionality of predicate verbs. Importantly, if the predicate of a clause is a volitional verb, then this marker cannot be used together with a first-person subject. Therefore, (73) below is ungrammatical.

(73) *ŋú   é-tso   ra
     1SG   DS-run   EVID:DIRECT
     Intended meaning: 'I ran downstream.'

Explaining why this clause is unacceptable, native speakers commented that this is because 'you cannot see yourself running.' However, they all agree that if one is watching a video recording of oneself running, then (73) can be said without any problem.

ra can occur freely with a first-person subject if the predicate verb is non-volitional (74a), or in a second-person declarative clause even if the predicate is volitional (74b) (Bai 2019: 237).

(74) a. ngɛ́   tə-ŋé   ra
        1SG+EXP   UP-be.ill EVID:DIRECT
        'I'm ill.'

     b. né   i   ŋú   le   té   kʰʁ-má-scŋa   ra
        2SG   ERG   1SG   DAT   at.all NONS-NEG-listen.to   EVID:DIRECT
        'You didn't listen to me at all.'

The direct evidential *ra* may originate from the motion verb which means 'go'. Aside from the fact that the two morphemes are homophonous, another piece of evidence for this claim is that *ra* 'go' cannot be followed by the direct evidential. One can say (75) if one has seen that a cow went downstream (Bai 2019: 238).

(75) ŋə́mo   tó-lö   a-rá
     cow   one-CLF:GENR   DS-go+EVID:DIRECT
     'A cow went downstream.'

In this example, *ra* takes the dual function of a motion verb and a direct evidential marker.

The inferential evidential auxiliary *sə* shows a three-way person-number inflection through vocalic change: *sö* for first-person singular, *sü* for second-person singular, and *se* for first or second person non-singular. This marker contrasts, both paradigmatically and functionally, with the imperfect marker *pi*, which also has a three-way inflection, and the afore-mentioned direct evidential *ra*. Thus it can either be analyzed as an aspect marker with an extended evidential sense [which is cross-linguistically quite common for perfects, see Aikhenvald (2004: 112) and Forker (2018)], or an evidential marker, as it also shows the first-person effects often found for non-firsthand evidentials (to be discussed shortly). For the purpose of this study, the second option is adopted.

This marker can only be used with dynamic verbs and for past situations. In terms of its evidential sense, it often indicates that the information is based on visual or non-visual sensory evidence or assumption. This function can be most clearly seen through comparison with the direct evidential *ra*, as in (76) (Bai 2019: 241).

(76) a. rɔ   té-zɛ   tʰó-sə   **ra**
       snake   one-CLF:LONG   TS-die   EVID:DIRECT
       'A snake died.'

   b. rɔ́   té-zɛ   tʰó-sə.   sə
       snake   one-CLF:LONG   TS-die   PFV
       'A snake died.'

(76a) implies that the speaker saw the whole process of the death of the snake. In contrast, if the speaker only saw a dead snake, she would use (76b), as she is inferring that the snake has died based on observable results (Bai 2019: 241).

As was mentioned above, this marker shows the first-person effects commonly found for non-firsthand, non-visual or reported evidentials. When used together with a first-person subject and a volitional predicate, this marker indicates lack of control or inadvertent action on the part of the speaker. Consider the example in (77) (Bai 2019: 249).

(77) ŋí   nbətʂá   tó-lö   ní-tʰɛ
     1SG+ERG   worm   one-CLF:GENR   DOWN-trample
     no-só   sö
     DOWN-kill   PFV.1SG
     'I stepped on a worm and killed it.'

This sentence implies that the speaker stepped on the worm unintentionally and may feel regretful after realizing that the worm was dead.

There are two ways to rephrase this sentence if the action is carried out consciously or on purpose. One way is to replace the inferential evidential marker with the narrow scope egophoric particle *ŋo*, the other is to add the wide scope egophoric marker *nyi* after the evidential marker, the difference being that the aspectual information is specified in the latter case but not in the first [see Bai (2019: 249) for more details].

When the predicate is non-volitional, then a first-person subject can occur naturally with the inferential evidential, as in (78).

(78) *məhú*   *ŋí*   *né*   *nó-mi*   *sö*
      last.night 1SG+ERG 2SG   DOWN-dream   PFV.1SG
      'I dreamed of you last night.'

The reported evidential marker *tə́pi* signals that the information source is hearsay. It consists of the verb *tə* 'say' and the imperfect aspect auxiliary *pi* (in third person form). It does not enter into the same paradigm with the direct evidential *ra* or the inferential evidential *sə*, and can be used after either of the two markers (79).

(79) *nɛ*   *ɣɛ*   *tə́-tsɔ*   *ra*   *tə́pi*
      2SG   EXP   UP-be.hungry   EVID:DIRECT   EVID:REP
      'It is said that you are hungry.'

If the author of the quoted report is specified, then the clause becomes either a direct or indirect speech report. In this case, *tə́pi* should be analyzed as a predicate verb plus an imperfect marker, not an evidential marker, as in (80).

(80) *otsí*   [*ɣɔ́sə*   *kʰɯ-tṣɛ́*   *po*
      3SG+ERG the.day.after.tomorrow NONS-arrive IMPF.1SG
      ŋo]   *tə́*   *pi*
      EGO   say   IMPF
      'He says "I will arrive the day after tomorrow."'

This is an example of direct speech report, as can be seen from the person marking on the imperfect aspect auxiliary in the complement clause, which inflects for the first person—a feature of the original speech. Here *tə́* 'say' and *pi* combine into a verb complex, functioning as the predicate of the matrix clause, not as an evidential marker. Since *tə́* 'say' is a transitive verb, the third person pronominal subject takes the ergative form. This indicates that in Munya, the reported evidential does not take the function of a quotative evidential.

Evidential markers are not obligatory in Munya. A clause that can be marked for evidentiality but nonetheless not formally marked can be considered evidentiality-neutral, that is, the specification of information source is not essential (cf. Aikhenvald 2018). The reported evidential is not obligatorily used in story-telling—while it occurs several times in a short story, in a much longer story it was used only once and in another it was not used at all.

The three evidential markers can all be used in interrogative clauses and negative clauses, but no evidential can be used in imperative clauses. When an evidential appears in an interrogative clause, it is the addressee's information source that is presupposed.

2.7 Ersu

There are three dialects of Ersu, which are Ersu Proper, Tosu, and Lizu (Zhang 2013: 2). Among these dialects, Tosu is virtually un-described and now almost extinct (Chirkova 2014), with only Ersu Proper and Lizu still being actively spoken. The two dialects are common in having an inferential evidential, a reported evidential, and a quotative evidential. While there is also a zero-marked direct evidential in Ersu Proper, the situation is unclear if a clause unmarked for non-direct evidentials indicates direct source of information or not in Lizu. Grammaticalization of the reported and quotative evidentials is still in progress in the two dialects. This can be seen from the fact that in Ersu Proper, the reported evidential and the quotative evidential have more than one forms which are similar to each other and can be used interchangeably. And in Lizu, the same form is used for both the reported and the quotative function.

2.7.1 Ersu Proper

Ersu has four evidentials, a direct evidential, which is formally unmarked, an inferential evidential, a reported evidential, and a quotative evidential. Overt evidential markers occur clause- or sentence-finally, after tense-aspect morphemes (Zhang 2014).

The direct evidential in Ersu is both formally and functionally unmarked. That is, if a clause does not take any evidential marker, it is understood that the information is obtained through direct evidence. Ersu direct evidential covers information acquired through any sensory perception, such as seeing (81a), hearing (81b), feeling (81c), smelling (81d) or generic knowledge (81e) (Zhang 2014).

(81) a. *sipu=tɕʰo   loɚ   tə   dzo*
       tree=LOC.SUPRESS turtledove INDEF   COP
       'There is a turtledove on the tree.'

b. *tṣʰo   tə   ə⊥=gə*
   dog   INDEF   bark=PROG
   'A dog is barking.'

c. *ta-ɳo   mɛtɕo   dzolo   da-tsʰa*
   present-day   sky   over   UP-be.hot
   'It is very hot today.'

d. *tʰə   ŋuà-ʂɨ̀=bɛ   tsɛ   də-xə*
   DEM   ox-meat=PL   really   UP-smell.good
   'This beef really smells good.'

e. *a⊥   ə⊥su=bɛ̀   tə-ɳo-ɳo   vùt-ɕò   də-tsu=gə*
   1PL.SLF   PN=PL   one-day-day   head-bind   UP-wear=PROG
   'We Ersu people wear a turban every day.'

If the information is acquired through inference or assumption, then the inferential evidential *=pà* would be obligatorily used. This marker is seldom attested in narratives, but can be frequently found in daily conversations. It can be used in a future situation, in which case it indicates the speaker's uncertainty, that is, it has epistemic overtones (Zhang 2014). The inference is based on tangible evidence in (82a) and logical reasoning in (82b) (Zhang 2014).

(82) a. *mɛtɕo   su-ɳo   tʰə-pʰu=gə=pà*
        sky   nex-day   TS-change=PROG=EVID:INFR
        'The weather is going to change tomorrow.' (The speaker makes this inference based on such evidence as the changes in the clouds, temperature, wind, etc.)

   b. *tʰə   nbo   tṣa   duá=pà*
      3SG.PREST   horse   search   go.PFV=EVID:INFR
      'He might have gone to search for his horse.' (The speaker went to someone's house, and found that the person was not at home at a particular time, for example, 5:00 pm when an Ersu often goes to drive their horses back home. They have this logical reasoning according to their general knowledge rather than evidence.)

The reported evidential markers *=dzě* and *=dzigə* (there is no semantic or functional difference between the two) indicate that the information is acquired through hearsay, as in (83).

(83)   tʰə   ya-no   kuaṣa   duá=dzě
        3SG.PREST   last-day   town   go.PFV=EVID:REP
        'It is said that he went to the town yesterday.'

There are several interchangeable variants of the quotative evidential marker in Ersu, which are all somewhat related to *dzi* 'say', a reconstructed form that is not attested in actual speech. According to Zhang (2014), the fact that there are so many variants may indicate that 'a "stable and mature" quotative evidential has not fully grammaticalized'. The example given in (84) comes from a traditional story. Note that the quotative markers are different in the two clauses and can be used interchangeably (Zhang 2014).

(84)   awa=nè,   'kʰa-la   ŋə-dzɿ=gə'=**dzɛ**;
        grandmother=TOP   IN-plough   OUT-eat=PROG=EVID:QUO
        apu=nè,   'na-ka   ŋə-dzɿ=gə'=**dza**
        grandfather=TOP   DOWN-kill   OUT-eat=PROG=EVID:QUO
        'The old lady said: "(The ox should be fed) to plough fields and provide food". The old man said: "(The ox should) be killed and eaten."'

There is no constraint on the co-occurrence of evidentials with aspects (Zhang 2013: 587) or with the types of verbs (Zhang 2014) in Ersu. However, the choice of certain evidentials seem to be correlated with speech genres (narrative vs. conversation) and person. The notion of 'person' here refers to speech act participants and non-speech act participants (Zhang 2014).

In the narrative genre, such as mythologies and folklore, the speech act participant is the narrator, with all other participants being the non-speech act participant. In this genre, clauses with a speech act participant tend to be marked with the direct evidential while those with a non-speech act participant are often marked with the quotative evidential (in the case of a first or second person participant) or reported evidential (in the case of a third person participant) (Zhang 2014). In the conversational genre, the speech act participants are the speaker and the addressee, and the non-speech act participant is the third person. When a conversation includes only the speaker and the addressee, 'since oral information transmission between the first and second person is always in a direct way, reported and quotative evidential are not applicable' (Zhang 2014), therefore only the direct and the inferential evidentials are found. With non-speech act participants, all evidentials can be used (Zhang 2014).

2.7.2 Lizu Dialect

Chirkova (2008) identifies two evidential markers in Lizu, an inferential evidential =dæ and a reported-cum-quotative evidential dʑige (cf. the reported evidential =dʑigə in Ersu Proper), and the two can be used in both past and present situations.[15]

The inferential evidential marker =dæ may have developed from the past form of dæ, which means 'go'. This marker indicates speakers' conjuncture of the event based on evidence gathered through sensory channel(s) or inference. In the two examples below, (85a) denotes an unaccomplished situation and (85b) an accomplished situation. In the second example, the evidential marker replaces the perfective marker æ.

(85) a. ^{L}ng^{w}æ ^{L}ʑe=^{H}læ ^{L}ge=^{L}dæ
rain   fall=come   NON.CTRL=EVID:INFR
'It seems like it is going to rain.'

b. ^{H}t^{h}e ^{L}ne-^{L}dzi=^{LH}dæ
3SG   DOWN-eat=EVID:INFR
'It seems like she has eaten.'

The reported-cum-quotative evidential dʑige indicates that the information is based on someone else's verbal account. The original speaker can either be stated or not. The marker consists of the quotative element dʑi 'speak' and the progressive-inchoative aspect marker ge (Chirkova 2008). (Recall that in §2.7.1, it was mentioned that dʑi cannot be used freely in Ersu.) An example is given in (86).

(86) ^{H}t^{h}e ^{H}jæ-^{H}x^{w}æ ^{H}æ-^{H}mæ ^{L}ne-^{L}je-^{LH}ma
3SG   past-evening   VOC-mother   DOWN-dream-see?.PST

---

15   She does not explicitly state whether in Lizu a clause not overtly marked for evidentiality has a direct evidential interpretation or not. In one place, she mentions that '[d]irect knowledge of the situation appears to be implied in most cases, and particularly in those where the control marker bo is used' (Chirkova 2008: 32), and in another place, that 'the speaker in Lizu can have direct knowledge only of those situations (either actual or planned), of which he is a participant and observer' (Chirkova 2008: 34). Thus she seems to believe that direct information can be implied in many situations, albeit with no concrete marking. However, in another place, she writes that, for clauses without the two evidential markers and the egophoric aspect marker bo, 'the source of information is simply unspecified, and can be either direct or indirect' (Chirkova 2008: 32). This seems to indicate that in Lizu a clause not formally marked for evidentiality does not have any fixed evidential value.

$^L dzi^L ge$
EVID:REP
'He says that he dreamt of his mother last night.'

2.8 Pumi

Pumi (a.k.a. Prinmi) is generally divided into a northern dialect and a southern dialect, each containing several varieties (Lu 2001).[16] According to Y. Jiang (2019), varieties in the northern dialect tend to have a firsthand evidential (*qinjian*) and a non-firsthand evidential (*feiqinjian*) in perfective contexts, and also a reported evidential. The firsthand evidential is in zero-form, and the non-firsthand evidential is marked with *sɿ*. The latter shows first-person effects, and may have developed from the perfective aspect. In contrast, there is no firsthand versus non-firsthand evidential distinction in the southern dialect. While the reported evidential is attested in both dialects, it is obligatory in the northern dialect but optional in the southern dialect.

This observation is largely corroborated by other works on Pumi. In the following discussion, we will mainly look at two varieties—the Niuwozi variety from the southern dialect (§2.8.1) and the Wadu variety from the northern dialect (§2.8.2).

2.8.1 Southern Dialect

Ding (2014: 210) identifies only one evidential in the Niuwozi variety of southern Pumi:[17] the reported evidential *tɕi*, which is grammaticalized from the verb *tɕi^R* 'to say'.[18] As an evidential marker, it has lost its verbal properties, such as the ability to take directional prefixes or to be negated or questioned. When functioning as an evidential, it does not stand alone, but needs to be followed by the imperfective, giving the form of *tɕi=ɿju*. Its evidential function is evident from the fact that it can appear after the speaking verb, as in (87) (Ding 2014: 210).

(87) $ne^L=njõ^H$ 3^L be^H $tʂ^he^R$ $ma^L=ɿwa^F$
      2SG=DSC+INS 1SG at feed NEG=willing.to.give
      gja^H $tɕi^L=si^L$ $tɕi^L ɿju^L$
      ATT   say=PFV   EVID:REP
      '"You are unwilling to feed me!" said (the Dragon Queen).'

---

16 A less popular classification, proposed by Ding (2014: 9), classifies the language into a western, a central, and a northern dialect.
17 Ding groups this variety to the central dialect. Based on the binary classification approach adopted here, it is seen as a southern dialect.
18 Ding (2014: 210) labels this as a quotative evidential. However, in none of the examples that he gives the original author of the reported information is overtly stated, hence it may be more appropriate to call it a reported evidential.

This evidential has an epistemic overtone, in the sense that the speaker can use it to distance himself from the statement being made, implying that he does not vouch for the veracity of the information, as in (88) (Ding 2014: 211).

(88) mja^{H}bu^F=ge^L=bo^L kʰə^{H}gjõ^L to^L nɜ^L-tṣwa^L=si^H tɕi^L.ju^L
     eyelid=TOP=FRM   knee   on   DOWN-contact=PFV   EVID:REP
     'It is said that their eyelids touch down to the knees.'

It also has certain mirative effect (89a), and can also be used for irony (89b) (Ding 2014: 21).

(89) a. pu^{H}ɕi^L ɜ^H ʑi^{H}me^L ti^L gə^L-tʃʰjõ^L ɜ^H xã^L ti^H
        last.night   1SG   dream   one   OUT-appear   1SG   parrot   one
        be^H tʰɜ^L-pʼaw^F=si^L tɕi^L.ju^L
        to   TS-transform=PFV   EVID:REP
        'Last night I dreamt of myself transforming into a parrot.'

   b. ni^F me^H=ɕi^H=ge^L la^L ɜ^L be^H da^H tɕi^L.ju^L,   ni^F
      3SG   NEG+PFV=go=TOP   also   1SG   at   blame   EVID:REP   3SG
      me^H=ɕi^H=ge^L ɜ^H me^{H}dzõ^L mã^{L}si^H jõ^L
      NEG+PFV=go=TOP   1SG   how   know   ASR
      'His not going is also blamed on me; how on earth should I know he wouldn't go?'

Omitting the quotative evidential in (89a) is infelicitous, as it would imply that what happened in the dream is true. Similarly, leaving out this evidential in (89b) would take away the irony tone and indicate that the speaker actually thinks that he should be blamed.

Similarly, in Dayang, another variety of the southern dialect, Y. Jiang (2015: 312) documents only a reported evidential, i.e. tʃə$^{24/31}$də$^{24/31}$. She also notes that certain motion verbs have suppletive forms that respectively express firsthand (qinjian) and non-firsthand (feiqinjian) meanings. For example, the firsthand and non-firsthand forms of 'come' are xa^{31}tʂhuŋ^{55} and ʑi$^{24/31}$, and those for 'go' are tə^{55}lo$^{24/55}$ and tə^{55}ɕi$^{24/31}$ (Y. Jiang 2015: 315).

2.8.2   Northern Dialect

In Wadu, a variety of northern Pumi, egophoricity and evidentiality form one paradigm, the choice of which is jointly determined by the verb semantics of control and the distinction between self-person and other-person (Daudey 2014a,b).

Daudey (2014a: 335) identifies five evidentials in this variety: an inferential evidential, a non-egophoric imperfective evidential, an auditory evidential, a hearsay evidential (renamed as 'reported evidential' here), and a reported thought evidential. She also mentions a zero-marked visual evidential in her discussion, but fails to include it in the evidential system. Not all the five evidentials recognized by her, however, meet the definition of evidentiality adopted in this study. In particular, the non-egophoric imperfective marker =ɖaw is used to describe other people's current or habitual actions, state a generally known fact, mark assertions concerning other people's internal states or qualities, or denote non-controllable actions (Daudey 2014a: 368–70). None of these seem to bear any direct relations to source of information, thus this marker is not considered as evidential in nature here. In a similar vein, the arguments for analyzing the reported thought marker *ɕi* as an evidential (Daudey 2014a: 388–9) are equally uncompelling, for its major function seems to be to introduce a complement clause, and is best seen as a kind of evidential strategy (cf. Aikhenvald 2018).

Therefore, in what follows I will only look at four categories in the evidential system of Wadu Pumi: the visual evidential, the inferential evidential, the auditory evidential, and the reported evidential.

There is a zero-marked visual evidential and an inferential evidential =*si*, which are only found in perfective contexts. The former indicates that the information is acquired through visual evidence (90a) and the latter marks source of information based on inference (90b) (Daudey 2014a: 361).

(90) a. *tɔ́   tɕʰĭ   qʰə̀-dzwɔ́*
    3SG   food   OUT-eat+PFV+NON.EGO
    'He has eaten.'

   b. *dăwmà   mí=tɕʰóŋ=sì*
      PN   NEG+PFV=come+PFV+NON.EGO=EVID:INFR
      'Dauma has not come back yet.'

In the case of self-person contexts with non-controllable verbs, the inferential =*si* needs to be used, the function of which is to denote unconsciousness (91a) or deferred realization (91b) (Daudey 2014a: 364–5). This means the inferential evidential in Wadu has first-person effects.

(91) a. *ébàw   nè-mɔ́=sì*
       INTERJ   DOWN-forget=EVID:INFR
       'My oh my! (I) forgot (everything).'

b. é   nè-gwé=sì
   1SG DOWN-drink=EVID:INFR
   'I am drunk.'

A mirative reading will arise if =si appears after stative verbs. This is used when one has just discovered that a situation is the case (Daudey 2014a: 365).

(92)ə́jù,   mə̀zæ̀ wé   mà-ɖǽ=sî,   mín   dzə̀?
     INTERJ bread make NEG-resemble=EVID:INFR what   be
     'Oh, the bread is very good, how come?'

This reminds us of the non-firsthand imperfective in Japhug Rgyalrong (§2.1.3) and the inferential evidential in Ronghong Qiang (§2.4.1).

Wadu Pumi also has an auditory evidential =tiŋ. This evidential is used when a speaker acquires his knowledge of a situation through what he hears, rather than sees or infers. The auditory stimuli can either be non-verbal sounds (93a) or overheard speech (93b) (Daudey 2014a: 380–1).

(93) a. qʰə̀-dzə́   kʰí=bù   də̀bǔ   m̥ə́=ɻə
        OUT-eat   time=TOP   then   person=PL
        tɕʰóŋ=tìŋ   tɕàw
        come+PFV+NON.EGO=EVID:AUD   EVID:REP
        '(...) after (he) had eaten, (he) heard people coming, it is said.'

    b. wútɕí ɻə́=nʲæ̀   ʂéj=tìŋ   bàw,   ɦàw,
       PN   first=just go+PFV+NON.EGO=EVID:AUD   CONTR   INTERJ
       ɦòŋ-dzí   tɕʰòŋʋ́óŋ=ɕíŋ   tɕə̀   ɦà   ʂéj=tìŋ
       in-location wait=VOL+PL   say   LNK go+PFV+NON.EGO=EVID:AUD
       '(...) (I) heard Wujin leave first, and heard (her) say: "We will wait up the valley," and leave.'

According to Daudey (2014a: 382), the auditory evidential may originate from an existential verb. As a verb, even though it cannot take directional prefixes, it can be preceded by an interrogative marker or a negator, as in (94) (Daudey 2014a: 382).

(94) m̥ə   mǎ=tîŋ
     person NEG=exist.EVID:AUD
     'There is no person.' (auditory evidence)

The reported evidential *tɕəɖaw* results from the grammaticalization of *tɕə̌* 'to say' and the non-egophoric imperfective marker =*ɖaw* into one morpheme. The two components have undergone even more phonological reduction in that they are often merged into *tɕaw*, as is shown in (95). *tɕəɖaw* and *tɕaw* are always interchangeable (Daudey 2014a: 385).

(95) iŋ-bú=bù,   ˌɟə̀-kʰí   kè   mə́dzə̀   tɕàw
      1PL+INCL-household=TOP front-time capable GN   EVID:REP
      'It is said that in the past our household was very capable.'

The reported evidential marker can be used twice in a sentence. This usage is demonstrated in (96), where it means that the story was passed down from a long time ago (Daudey 2014a: 386–7).

(96) pédí=bì   dəbǔ   nə́   tɕwə́=sì
      toad=DAT   then   thus   say+PFV+NON.EGO=EVID:INFR
      tɕàw   tɕàw
      EVID:REP   EVID:REP
      '(…) (he) said this to the toad, it is said, it is said. (…)'

The reported evidential is also used to indicate that speakers do not vouch for the truth of what they are reporting. It is also used to report one's dream, as in (97) (Daudey 2014a: 387–8).

(97) é   pón   dzə́   tɕə̀ɖàw
      1SG   official be   EVID:REP
      'I am a king.'

2.9   Guiqiong

As an endangered Qiangic language spoken in a restricted area, Guiqiong has no dialects. By far the most thorough discussion on its evidential system is in L. Jiang (2015: 248–58).[19]

L. Jiang (2015: 248) recognizes four evidential constructions in Guiqiong, which are the visual evidential marker -*ʂu'wu*, the experienced auditory evidential marker -*tsimu* (renamed as 'experienced reported evidential'), the

---

19   Song (2018), a paper that purportedly deals with evidentiality in Guiqiong, defines evidentiality as 'the degree of the reliability of information'. It is thus irrelevant to the present study.

gnomic auditory evidential marker -*tsi'wu* (renamed as 'gnomic reported evidential'), and the speculative mood marker -*əmu*-. Treating the speculative mood as a kind of evidential category is confusing at best, and it is better seen as a kind of mood, as the name suggests. In addition, L. Jiang (2015: 109) also mentions a hearsay evidential (renamed as 'reported evidential') particle *tsi*, which should also be included in the system. The evidentiality system to be presented below thus consists of a visual evidential, a reported evidential, an experienced reported evidential and a gnomic reported evidential.

The visual evidential marker -*ṣu'wu* consists of the verb *ṣu* 'be true' and the gnomic tense marker -*'wu*. According to L. Jiang (2015: 254), 'the speaker does not use this marker to guarantee the truth or preciseness of his or her statement, but to disclose a visual impression', as in (98) (L. Jiang 2015: 254).

(98)   zo   'lo-ɲyeŋ-ṣu'wu
       3SG   read-can-EVID:VIS
       'It seems that he can read.'

This marker can also be used to express simile, as in (99) (L. Jiang 2015: 255).

(99)   khu   tɕieŋkɛi   yəu-ṣu'wu
       dog   wolf   resemble-EVID:VIS
       'The dog looks like a wolf.'

The reported evidential particle *tsi* indicates that the situation denoted by the sentence is a matter of hearsay. It is grammaticalized from the verb that means listen, hear and say. An example is given in (100) (L. Jiang 2015: 109).

(100) dɛi   mũ-pɛi   tṣhi   gɛ   tsi
       this   person-CLF   very   be.good   EVID:REP
       'It is said that that person is very good.'

The experienced reported evidential -*tsimu* is grammaticalized from the speech report verb *tsi* in combination with the present tense marker of experienced perceptions *mu*, which marks an occurrence the speaker has just experienced. It does not warrant the exact content of what the speaker has heard of. An example is given in (101) (L. Jiang 2015: 248–9).

(101) zo   gutɕie   ji-'wu-**tsimu**
       3SG   PN   go-GN-EVID:EREP
       'I heard that he is going to Gūzán.'

The gnomic reported evidential marker -*tsi'wu* contains the causative directive marker -*tsi* and the gnomic tense marker -*'wu*. The directive causative marker -*tsi* is also grammaticalized from the verb of speaking. As a directive causative marker, however, it is used to report on requests and orders that the speaker has received. A speaker uses this marker to disclose what he hears of to the addressee, who is not supposed to know about the situation before (L. Jiang 2015: 249–50). Consider (102) below (L. Jiang 2015: 250).

(102)   ŋə   go-*tsi'wu*
        1SG eat-EVID:GREP
        '(I don't think you know this.) He asks me to eat.'

In (102), the speaker was asked by someone else to have his dinner. The addressee has no knowledge of the request so far. When the speaker sat at the table to eat, he explained to the addressee that he did so on the request by somebody else.

2.10   *Shixing*

With around only 18,00 speakers, Shixing is another critically endangered language (Chirkova 2009). The nature of evidentiality in Shixing remains elusive, partly because the language is still poorly described, partly because there are different views on whether or not certain grammatical markers should be analyzed as evidentials.

B. F. Huang and Renzeng (1991) [cited in Chirkova (2009)] recognize two evidentials in Shixing: *tɕæ* signals that the speaker has witnessed the event or process denoted by the verb, and *wu* and *dzõ* together indicate that the speaker has witnessed the outcome of the event or process denoted by the verb. However, Chirkova (2009) analyzes *tɕæ* as a mirative marker, on the grounds that '[i]ts function appears to be to signal contexts in which the speaker's discovery of the reported situation is recent, consequently expressing surprise, unexpectedness, unprepared mind and new knowledge.' Furthermore, she analyzes *wu* as a resultative aspect marker and *dzõ* as a durative aspect marker, with the former signaling that a state or an event exists as a result of a transition in the past, and the latter denoting present situations that are in effect or in progress. In view of these controversies, I refrain from making conclusions on the evidential systems in Shixing at the present stage.

3 Discussion

This section will first summarize the findings that can be made from the above discussion, by concluding that the evidentiality systems in Qiangic languages can be grouped into three types (§3.1), then explore whether these evidentiality systems are inherited from Proto-Qiang or arose through independent grammaticalization (§3.2), and finally look at the theoretical implications that can be derived from the direct evidential and the reported evidential (§3.3).

3.1 *Three Types of Evidentiality Systems*

The evidentiality systems of the Qiangic languages discussed above are summarized in Table 3.1. Based on the currently available data, we can identify three recurrent types of evidential systems in Qiangic languages. Type A, represented by Rgyalrongic languages, is characterized by a two-term subsystem in the past tense, which consists of a firsthand evidential and a non-firsthand evidential, with the firsthand zero-marked. The other subsystem tends to contain a reported evidential and/or a direct evidential, as are cases of Wobzi Khroskyabs, Jiaomuzu Rgyalrong, Japhug Rgyalrong and Rtau Horpa. Cogtse Rgyalrong is special in that it has another two-term subsystem in the present tense.

Type B, which is commonly found in varieties of Qiang, consists of a visual, an inferential and a reported evidential. An important feature of this type of system is that the visual evidential is either optionally marked, as in Ronghong and Longxi, or zero-marked, as in Puxi. Aside from these three exponents, Qugu Qiang in addition has a predictive evidential and an assumed evidential.

Somewhat similar to Type B, Type C contains a direct evidential, an inferential evidential, and a reported evidential. Certain languages may in addition have a quotative evidential. Languages or varieties belonging to this type are nDrapa, Munya, Ersu Proper, and interestingly, Geshiza Horpa, a Rgyalrongic language. With an extra auditory evidential, the system of Wadu Pumi can be seen as a variant of this type.

Finally, there are three languages/varieties that cannot be grouped into any of these three types: Niuwozi Pumi only has a reported evidential, Lizu Ersu has an inferential and a reported-cum-quotative evidential, and Guiqiong has a visual evidential and a reported evidential that contrasts three functions.

3.2 *Evidentiality in Qiangic: Genetic Retention or Independent Development?*

A natural question that arises at this juncture is whether the evidentiality systems found in these Qiangic languages are inherited from Proto-Qiang—

TABLE 3.1 A summary of the evidentiality systems in Qiangic languages

Language	Evidentiality system
Rgyalrong	
Situ dialect	
Cogtse variety	two firsthand versus non-firsthand subsystems, one in the past tense, one in the present; past tense: firsthand marked with ∅, non-firsthand◦ with vocalic change; present tense: firsthand with *na-*, non-firsthand with *ŋa-*
Jiaomuzu variety	firsthand (∅) and non-firsthand◦ (-*'a*) in the past tense, reported (*kacəs*), observational★ (*'na-~'nə-*)
Japhug dialect	
Kamnyu variety	firsthand (∅) and non-firsthand◦★ (directional prefix or *pɯ-/pjɤ-*) in the past tense, direct★ (*ɲɯ-*), factual (∅) and reported (*khi*)
Khroskyabs	
Core Khroskyabs	
Wobzi variety	firsthand (∅) and non-firsthand◦★ (=*si*) in the past tense, reported (-*rǽ*)
Horpa	
Central dialect	
Rtau variety	firsthand (∅) and non-firsthand (-*sə*) in the past tense, direct (-*rə*)
Geshiza variety	direct (-*ræ*), inferential◦★(-*sʰi*), reported (-*jə*), quotative (-*wo*)
Qiang	
Northern dialect	
Ronghong variety	visual◦ (-(*w*)*u*), inferential◦★ (-*k*), reported (-*i*)
Qugu variety	visual (-*w*), inferential★ (-*k*), predictive (-*ji-jy*), assumed (-*tɕi*), reported (-*ji*)
Southern dialect	
Puxi variety	visual (∅), inferential (-*ba*), reported (-*u*)
Longxi variety	visual (=*tɕʰi*), inferential (=*wù*), reported (=*ɤ̆ʮ*)
nDrapa	
Upper dialect	direct (∅), inferential (=*ba*), reported (=*dɛ*)
Lower dialect	direct (-*ʂtr*^{33}), inferential (-*mba*^{33}), reported (-*dɛ*^{33}/-*dɛ*^{33}*dzɛ*^{33}, -*dɛ*^{33}*dzḛ*^{33} and -*dzɛ*^{33}*dɛ*^{33}), quotative (-*dɛ*^{33})
Munya	
Northern dialect	direct (*ra*), inferential◦ (*sə*), reported (*təpi*)

TABLE 3.1   A summary of the evidentiality systems in Qiangic languages (cont.)

Language	Evidentiality system
Ersu	
Ersu Proper	direct (∅), inferential (=pà), reported (=dzě or =dzigə), quotative (=dzɛ or =dza)
Lizu dialect	inferential (=dæ), reported-quotative (dzige)
Pumi	
Southern dialect	
Niuwozi variety	reported⋆ (tʂɿju)
Northern dialect	
Wadu variety	visual (∅), inferential∘⋆ (=si), auditory (=tiŋ), reported (tɕəɖaw ~tɕaw)
Guiqiong	visual (-ʂu'wu), reported (tsi, tsimu and tsi'wu)

∅: evidential marked in zero-form
∘: evidential shows first-person effects
⋆: evidential has mirative overtones

assuming that these languages are genetically affiliated—or arose independently, following common grammaticalization paths attested across languages. To answer this question, we need to consider if there are any similarities in these systems, and if so, what are their possible origins. These similarities can be looked at from three aspects, which are similarities in the form of evidential markers, similarities in the organization of evidential systems, and similarities in the meanings or functions of particular evidentials, especially their extensions and overtones.

The evidential markers that are similar in both form and function found across Qiangic languages (not just in dialects or varieties within one language) are given in Table 3.2.

The evidential that has the greatest likelihood of being traceable to Proto-Qiang is an inferential evidential, which is attested in four languages (including two varieties of Horpa) and probably consisted of a voiceless alveolar fricative and a high front vowel (*si). In all these languages/varieties, this marker is restricted to past or perfective situations. And in Munya, this evidential can be alternatively analyzed as a perfective aspect with extended evidential meanings. Thus, while it is possible that this marker acted as an inferential evidential in Proto-Qiang, it might also just be a past tense or perfective/perfect aspect marker at that stage, with the evidential function independently developed after these languages split. This kind of grammaticalization, where

TABLE 3.2 Evidential markers with similar forms and functions in Qiangic languages

Inferential evidential 1				
Wobzi Khroskyabs	Rtau Horpa	Geshiza Horpa	Northern Munya	Wadu Pumi
=si	-sə	-sʰi	sə	=si
Inferential evidential 2				
Puxi Qiang	Upper nDrapa	Lower nDrapa	Ersu Proper	
-ba	=ba	-mba³³	=pà	
Direct evidential				
Rtau Horpa	Geshiza Horpa	Northern Munya		
-rə	-rœ	ra		

a perfect, a past tense, and other forms with a completive meaning acquiring an additional overtone of inferred information and then developing into an inferential evidential, is well-documented across languages (cf. Aikhenvald 2004: 279, 2015).

Another inferential evidential with a more restricted distribution is found in three languages. This marker has a bilabial stop consonant and a low back vowel. For the purpose of discussion we will temporarily assume it to be *ba. Different from *si, *ba can be used in non-past situations, as in Lower nDrapa (§2.5.2) and Ersu (§2.7.1). It is similar in form and meaning to the Chinese clause final particle *pa* and also the Amdo Tibetan *ba* (Sandman 2016: 173), a major function of which is to denote uncertainty, used if a statement is made based on assumption or speculation. This similarity leads some researchers to hypothesize that it may be borrowed (e.g. Y. Huang 2019b). In fact, markers of similar form and function are also reported in several other Qiangic languages, albeit they are not analyzed as evidentials, but as epistemic modalities. In Mawo Qiang, a clause final particle, *γba*, is used for inference and speculation (Liu 1998: 203). In Wadu Pumi, the clause-final speculative marker *bǎ* 'denotes uncertainty about a situation' (Daudey 2014a: 397). In Geshiza Horpa, 'the probabilitative enclitic =ba "probably" functions as an indicator of uncertainty when the speaker is not completely sure of the veracity of a statement' (Honkasalo 2019: 575). Inspired by Sandman (2016: 173), Honkasalo hypothesizes that it may be borrowed from Tibetan. In Munya, the clause-final particle *pa* can denote possibility and roughly means 'maybe' (Bai 2019: 153). Thus, if we assume that this marker was borrowed, be it from Chinese or Tibetan, it would imply that there is no such evidential in Proto-Qiang. On the other hand, if we hypothesize that *ba existed in Proto-Qiang, then a more plausible scenario would be that it acted as an epistemic modality. This is because cross-linguistically, it is quite common for an epistemic modality to develop into an evidential (Aikhenvald 2015), and that in Qiangic languages this marker is an epistemic modality in some languages but has taken on the function of an evidential in others. This means there is not enough evidence to postulate *ba as an inferential evidential in Proto-Qiang.

The last evidential in the table is a direct evidential attested in two different languages. Recall that in Rtau and Geshiza, this evidential is only used in non-past situations and denotes information acquired from sensory and endopathic channels. While the direct evidential in Munya has a similar function, it is only used in perfective (for dynamic verbs) and genomic (for stative verbs) situations. Considering that this marker is found in such a restricted number of cases, and that it behaves differently with respect to tense-aspect in these two languages, arguing that it existed as an evidential in Proto-Qiang is problematic.

Next we consider the similarities in the organization of the evidentiality systems. Firstly, the overall structure of the systems within Rgyalrongic languages demonstrates that evidentiality in these languages cannot be inherited from a proto-language. Although these languages are similar in having a firsthand and non-firsthand subsystem in the past tense, the marked, non-firsthand evidentials are realized differently—with directional prefixes (or vocalic changes therein) in Core Rgyalrong but with a suffix/enclitic in Wobzi Khroskyabs and Rtau Horpa. Also, the condition for coding the non-firsthand evidential with (erstwhile) directional prefixes is that they must develop the perfective aspect function, as are the cases of the three varieties of Core Rgyalrong. Recall that in §2.2, Lai shows that directional prefixes do not have evidential functions. This is expected, considering the fact that directional prefixes in that language do not indicate perfectiveness, thus precluding them from further developing into non-firsthand evidentials. This grammaticalization path can be schematically represented as 'directional prefix → perfective aspect → non-firsthand evidential' [see also Lai (2017: 505)]. There is a cross-linguistic tendency for directional terms to develop the perfectivizing meaning (Bybee and Dahl 1989), and, as has been mentioned above, the development from a perfective to a non-firsthand or inferential evidential is also well-documented. These suggest that the firsthand and non-firsthand evidential subsystem in Rgyalrongic languages is likely to be independently developed, following the cross-linguistically common grammaticalization path.

Secondly, the prevalence of Type B and Type C systems among non-Rgyalrongic languages cannot be taken as evidence for their common origin. Typological studies have shown that the most commonly found evidentiality system is a tripartite system of a visual/direct evidential, an inferential evidential, and a reported evidential (Willett 1988; Aikhenvald 2004: 66). This is also the most widespread evidential systems in Qiangic languages, which covers both Type B and Type C systems discussed in §3.1. Therefore, there is the possibility that Type B and Type C systems arose from parallel development, and not necessarily through inheritance.

Furthermore, the forms of the reported or quotative evidential in these languages clearly show that this evidential is independently developed in each language. Virtually all researchers noticed that the reported or quotative evidential(s) in their languages grammaticalized from verbs of speech, as can be seen from the fact that the forms of the evidential and the verb are either identical or closely related. However, the speech report verbs and the reported or quotative evidentials differ dramatically among these languages (see Table 3.1). These indicate that the reported or quotative evidentials developed relatively recently in Qiangic languages.

Finally, we turn to the extensions and overtones of certain evidentials in Qiangic languages. As can be seen from Table 3.1, for many languages, the non-firsthand or inferential evidentials either show first-person effects (Kamnyu Rgyalrong, Munya), or the mirative overtone (Qugu Qiang), or both (Geshiza Horpa, Ronghong Qiang, Wadu Pumi). Such extensions are also sparsely found for other evidentials. In Kamnyu Rgyalrong, the direct evidential has a mirative function; in Ronghong Qiang, the visual evidential can be used for first-person effects; and in Niuwozi Pumi, the reported evidential also denotes mirativity. Again, such similarities in semantic extensions cannot be taken as evidence for the common origin of evidentiality in Proto-Qiang, as it is found that, cross-linguistically, a non-firsthand evidential tend to gain first-person effects (Aikhenvald 2004: 220), and mirative overtones are likely to be associated with the inferential or the reported term in languages with three or four evidentials (Aikhenvald 2004: 200).

In summary, while various levels of resemblances can be observed in the evidentiality systems across Qiangic languages, upon closer inspection, none of these similarities can be adduced as conclusive evidence for the common descent of the synchronic systems. For many apparent similarities, there is always the possibility that they arose from parallel development, following well-established paths of grammaticalization or semantic extension. On the contrary, evidence such as the two-term subsystems in varieties of Core Rgyalrong and the forms of reported evidentials strongly indicate that modern systems represent a recent development rather than common inheritance.

3.3 Theoretical Implications

The discussion in the previous section showed that many aspects of the evidentiality systems in Qiangic conform to well-attested typological tendencies of evidentiality. This does not mean, however, that the systems in this language group cannot shed new light on our understanding of evidentiality. In this section, we will look at two typologically unusual features of evidentiality recurrent in certain Qiangic languages—the special behaviors of the direct evidentials (§3.3.1) and the uncommon composition of the reported and quotative evidentials (§3.3.2).

3.3.1 The Special Properties of the Direct Evidential

Cross-linguistically, the direct evidential generally covers information obtained through sensory channels, such as seeing, hearing, smell and taste—that is, the parameters of (I) and (II) given in §1.3.1. Extensions of this evidential include speakers' certainty of what they are talking about, full control of the information, or full responsibility for the provided information (Aikhenvald 2004: 159–62). However, in several Qiangic languages—and Tibetic languages as well—the overtly marked direct evidential tends to show some unusual properties in terms of semantics and interactions with person.[20] In fact, this has already been noticed by Aikhenvald (2004: 230), who points out that '[t]his semantic property of the direct evidential in Amdo Tibetan and in Qiang is thus markedly different from direct and visual evidentials in other multiterm systems.' Augmented by data from other Qiangic languages, the following discussion can be seen as an elaboration on this insight.

Firstly, while all these direct evidentials cover visual and non-visual sensory information, they are also used for information based on speakers' own endopathic experiences, i.e. parameter (III). This is the case for Kamnyu Rgyalrong, Rtau Horpa, Geshiza Horpa, Munya, and Tibetic languages such as Standard Spoken Tibetan (Tournadre and Jiatso 2001) and Amdo Tibetan (J. T.-S. Sun 1993). Instead of having the canonical semantic extensions of certainty and control as mentioned above, they show unusual features, such as the mirative effect in Kamnyu (§2.1.3).

A more crucial property of these direct evidentials is that they cannot freely occur with first-person volitional actors. This is diametrically opposite to direct evidentials found in other language families, which expresses speakers' direct

---

20 Unmarked direct evidentials, such as those in Ersu Proper and Upper nDrapa, do not show these properties. A tentative explanation for this divergence is that the unmarked evidentials in these two languages may arise through more common grammaticalization pathways, while the Qiangic/Tibetic direct evidentials come about via parallel development. Although Lower nDrapa also has a direct evidential, it is not discussed here due to insufficiency of data.

knowledge and have overtones of certainty or control. However, if the predicate is an endopathic verb, such as 'to be hungry' or 'to miss someone', then this evidential becomes compatible with first-person actors. (For illustrations on this point, see the data from Munya in §2.6.)

Interestingly, special semantic effects can arise if this evidential is used with first-person volitional actors. (Not to be confused with the first-person effects found for non-firsthand or inferential evidentials.) Citing the data in Ronghong Qiang [example (37) in §2.4.1] and Amdo Tibetan (J. T.-S. Sun 1993), Aikhenvald (2004: 228) points out that in a few Tibeto-Burman languages, the visual or direct evidential with first person agents can imply that the action was carried out unintentionally or by mistake. To this we may add Taku Tibetan, where use of the direct evidential with a first-person volitional actor signals that the action was carried out by accident (J. T.-S. Sun 2018). This, however, is not the only possible semantic effect. Data from Munya and Standard Spoken Tibetan show that the semantic overtone can also be self-observation. Recall that example (73), from Munya, is normally unacceptable, but it becomes felicitous if the speaker utters this sentence while watching a video of herself running. In other words, using the direct evidential with a first-person volitional participant in Munya indicates that the speaker acts as an observer of her own action from the perspective of an outsider. Along similar lines, in Standard Spoken Tibetan, 'the sensorial or direct auxiliaries *song* and *'dug* are not normally used with the first person since they would imply self-observation. However, they occur in special situations when the speaker sees, or saw, himself in a movie, a dream, etc.' (Tournadre and Jiatso 2001).

These special semantic effects throw new light on the nature of these typologically unusual direct evidentials, which clearly go beyond simply marking direct information source. Explaining why the direct evidential tends to be used with non-volitional predicates in Amdo Tibetan, J. T.-S. Sun (1993) states that '[s]ince, however, these non-volitional acts were not under control by the speaker's will, the direct evidential $=t^h\alpha$ is used to indicate that he was merely a passive participant or witness of the portrayed events.' This captures the essence of the Qiangic/Tibetic direct evidentials, the primary meaning of which is non-volitional action and/or out-bound observation, with the secondary function of information source marking. Out-bound observation is directed towards the outside world, through all sensory channels—this is what we see when this evidential is used in non-first person contexts. Less commonly, the speaker can also observe herself—not through introspection, but by taking the perspective of an outsider, as in cases of watching a video of oneself or telling a dream. More situations of self-observation could be encountered as more research on this topic are carried out in the future.

TABLE 3.3   The interactions between first-person actor, volitionality and egophoric/alterphoric

	Egophoric	Alterphoric
First-person volitional actor	Volitional and conscious action	Special semantic effects: unintentional action or self-observation
First-person non-volitional actor	Special semantic effects: purposeful action	Non-volitional states, actions, and endopathic processes

The above discussion seems to show these unusual direct evidentials are more appropriately analyzed as a category that is opposite to egophoricity. Borrowing the terminology from Post (2013), it may be termed as 'alterphoric'. This kind of opposition can be represented in Table 3.3. (For the purpose of this study, only the first-person statement context is considered.)

This table essentially predicts that the default and canonical syntactic and semantic composition is for the first-person volitional actor to combine with egophoric marking and the first-person non-volitional actor with alterphoric marking. The first combination yields the egophoric reading, which involves volitional and conscious action. The second combination gives the alterphoric meaning, i.e. non-volitional states, actions and endopathic feelings or experiences. Special semantic effects arise when this distribution is skewed. Thus, when an alterphoric marker co-occurs with a first-person volitional actor, the overtones can be unintentional action or self-observation, which have been treated above. The other non-canonical composition, with first-person non-volitional actor going together with egophoric marking, is not abundantly discussed, but does occur. For example, in Amdo Tibetan, when the egophoric-like $=nə$ combines with 'verbs denoting bodily functions which are usually not initiated by volition', such as 'to yawn', 'to cough', and 'to sneeze', the connotation is that the speaker executes these actions on purpose or in an exaggerated way (J. T.-S. Sun 1993). Similarly, in Wadu Pumi, there is a 'control-adding' construction which consists in adding the light verb *pú* 'to do' after a non-controllable verb. The action is then portrayed as controllable and purposeful, allowing for the occurrence of the egophoric marker and the first-person actor (Daudey 2014b).

In a nutshell, it is possible to analyze the unusual direct evidential found in certain Qiangic and Tibetic languages as a category that is functionally opposite to egophoricity. This would allow for a more natural explanation for the peculiar behaviors and unexpected semantic extensions of this category.

3.3.2 Grammaticalization of the Reported and Quotative Evidentials

The reported and quotative evidentials in Qiangic languages should also be highlighted, for its unusual composition. Cross-linguistically, markers of reported and quotative evidential often come from a grammaticalized verb of speech (Aikhenvald 2004: 271). The speech verb can, in some cases, combine with other elements during the process of grammaticalization. For example, in many varieties of South American Spanish and Brazilian Portuguese, a verb of speech combined with a complementizer is gradually developing into a reported evidential marker (Alcázar 2018). The scenario is different in Qiangic languages, where a number of reported and quotative evidentials originate from a speech verb combined with a non-perfective aspect or a non-past tense marker. This is only observed in southern Qiangic languages, as only in these languages is aspect expressed periphrastically, that is, marked after main verbs. In Rgyalrongic languages and varieties of Qiang, aspects are expressed via verbal prefixes, which is unconducive for such kind of combination.

Languages with this kind of reported or quotative evidentials include Munya, Ersu Proper, the Lizu dialect of Ersu, Southern Pumi, Northern Pumi, and Guiqiong. In Munya, the reported evidential *tə́pi* is composed of the speech reported verb *tə́* and the imperfective aspect *pi* (§2.6). In Ersu Proper, the reported-cum-quotative evidential *dziɡə* consists of the verb *dzi* 'say' and the progressive/prospective aspect marker *ɡə* (Zhang 2014). This evidential is likely to be cognate with $^L dzi^L ɡe$ in the Lizu dialect, which has an identical function. Here *ɡe* is analyzed as a progressive-inchoative aspect marker (§2.7.2). In Southern Pumi, when functioning as a reported evidential, the speech report verb also needs to be followed by the imperfective aspect, giving the form of $tʃt^L ɹju^L$ (§2.8.1). In Northern Pumi, the reported evidential *tɕədaw* results from the grammaticalization of *tɕə́* 'to say' and the non-egophoric imperfective marker =*daw*, and can be further reduced into one syllable, as *tɕaw* (§2.8.2). Finally, in Guiqiong, the experienced reported evidential -*tsimu* consists of the verb *tsi* 'hear, listen, say' and the present tense marker of experienced perceptions *mu*, and the gnomic reported evidential marker -*tsi'wu* is composed of the causative directive marker -*tsi* and the gnomic tense marker -*'wu* (§2.9).

The motivation behind this pattern of composition, i.e. with a speech report verb and a non-perfective (typically an imperfective) or non-past tense marker, is not totally clear to me. Maybe because in Qiangic languages, the information acquired through hearsay is deemed to be timeless or held to be true at the time it is reported (which can be roughly paraphrased as 'people are saying that …' or 'people say that …'), and this prompts the use of the non-perfective or non-past tense markers. This erstwhile periphrastic construction then became entrenched and grammaticalized into one evidential marker.

4 Summary

This study examined the evidentiality systems in sixteen varieties of nine Qiangic languages within the classical framework developed by Aikhenvald. These systems can be grouped into three types: the Rgyalrongic type, which features for a firsthand and a non-firsthand subsystem in the past tense, the Qiang type, which has a visual, an inferential and a reported evidential, and the southern Qiangic type, which consists of a direct, an inferential, and a reported and/or a quotative evidential.

A thorough comparison of these systems show that they are unlikely to be inherited from a proto-language, but seem to be independently developed. One formally similar inferential evidential (*si*) found in several languages may originally acted as a past tense or perfective/perfect aspect marker, and the other (*pa*) can be optionally analyzed as an epistemic mood particle. The organization of the system in the Rgyalrongic group and the composition of reported and/or quotative evidentials indicate that they arose through parallel development. Similarities in the overall structure of the Qiang and the southern Qiangic types are typologically common.

This study also proposed a new analysis for the unusual direct evidential documented in certain Tibetic and Qiangic languages, arguing that it is more natural to see it as alterphoric, a category that is functionally opposite to egophoric. It also pointed out a special feature of the composition of the reported evidential recurrent in several Qiangic languages, which consists of a speech report verb and a non-perfective aspect or a non-past tense marker.

References

Aikhenvald, Alexandra Y. *Evidentiality*. Oxford: Oxford University Press, 2004.
Aikhenvald, Alexandra Y. "The essence of mirativity". In: *Linguistic Typology* 16 (2012), pp. 435–485. doi: 10.1515/lingty-2012-0017.
Aikhenvald, Alexandra Y. "The grammar of knowledge: A cross-linguistic view of evidentials and the expression of information source". In: *The grammar of knowledge*. Ed. by Alexandra Y. Aikhenvald and R. M. W. Dixon. New York: Oxford University Press, 2014, pp. 1–51.

Aikhenvald, Alexandra Y. "Evidentials: Their links with other grammatical categories". In: *Linguistic Typology* 19.2 (2015), pp. 239–277. doi: 10.1515/lingty-2015-0008.

Aikhenvald, Alexandra Y. "Evidentiality: The framework". In: *The Oxford handbook of evidentiality*. Ed. by Alexandra Y. Aikhenvald. Oxford: Oxford University Press, 2018, pp. 1–43.

Aikhenvald, Alexandra Y. *The web of knowledge: Evidentiality at the cross-roads*. Leiden: Brill, 2021.

Aikhenvald, Alexandra Y. and R. M. W. Dixon, eds. *Studies in evidentiality*. Amsterdam/Philadelphia: John Benjamins Publishing Company, 2003.

Alcázar, Asier. "Dizque and other emergent evidential forms in Romance languages". In: *The Oxford handbook of evidentiality*. Ed. by Alexandra Y. Aikhenvald. New York: Oxford University Press, 2018, pp. 726–741.

Bai, Jun Wei. "A grammar of Munya". PhD thesis. James Cook University, 2019.

Bai, Jun Wei. "Northern and southern Munya dialects: Towards a historical perspective". In: *Studia Linguistica* 75.2 (Aug. 2021), pp. 328–344.

Bybee, Joan L. and Östen Dahl. "The creation of tense and aspect systems in the languages of the world". In: *Studies in Language* 13.1 (1989), pp. 51–103.

Chafe, Wallace and Johanna Nichols, eds. *Evidentiality: The linguistic coding of epistemology*. New Jersey: Ablex Publishing Corporation, 1986.

Chirkova, Katia. "Essential characteristics of Lizu, a Qiangic language of Western Sichuan [Paper presentation]". In: *Workshop on Tibeto-Burman Languages of Sichuan*. Taipei, Dec. 2008.

Chirkova, Katia. "Shixing, a Sino-Tibetan language of south-west China: A grammatical sketch with two appended texts". In: *Linguistics of the Tibeto-Burman Area* 32.1 (Apr. 2009), pp. 1–89.

Chirkova, Katia. "The Qiangic subgroup from an areal perspective: A case study of languages of Muli". In: *Language and Linguistics* 13 (2012), pp. 133–170.

Chirkova, Katia. "The Duoxu Language and the Ersu-Lizu-Duoxu relationship". In: *Linguistics of the Tibeto-Burman Area* 37.1 (2014), pp. 104–146. doi: 10.1075/ltba.37.1.04chi.

Daudey, Henriëtte. "A Grammar of Wadu Pumi". PhD thesis. La Trobe University, 2014.

Daudey, Henriëtte. "Volition and control in Wadu Pumi". In: *Linguistics of the Tibeto-Burman Area* 37 (2014), pp. 75–103. doi: 10.1075/ltba.37.1.03dau.

DeLancey, Scott. "Evidentiality and volitionality in Tibetan". In: *Evidentiality: The linguistic coding of epistemology*. Ed. by Wallace Chafe and Johanna Nichols. New Jersey: Ablex Publishing Corporation, 1986, pp. 203–213.

DeLancey, Scott. "Mirativity: The grammatical marking of unexpected information". In: *Linguistic Typology* 1 (1997), pp. 33–52.

DeLancey, Scott. "Evidentiality in Tibetic". In: *The Oxford handbook of evidentiality*. Ed. by Alexandra Y. Aikhenvald. Oxford: Oxford University Press, 2018, pp. 580–609.

Ding, Picus Sizhi. *A grammar of Prinmi: Based on the central dialect of northwest Yunnan, China*. Leiden: Brill, 2014.

Evans, Nicholas, Henrik Bergqvist, and Lila San Roque. "The grammar of engagement I: Framework and initial exemplification". In: *Language and Cognition* 10.1 (Nov. 2017), pp. 110–140. doi: 10.1017/langcog.2017.21.

Floyd, Simeon, Elisabeth Norcliffe, and Lila San Roque, eds. *Egophoricity*. Amsterdam/Philadelphia: John Benjamins Publishing Company, 2018.

Forker, Diana. "Evidentiality and its relations with other verbal categories". In: *The Oxford handbook of evidentiality*. Ed. by Alexandra Y. Aikhenvald. Oxford: Oxford University Press, 2018, pp. 65–84. doi: 10.1093/oxfordhb/9780198759515.013.3.

Gawne, Lauren. "Egophoric evidentiality in Bodish languages". In: *Evidential systems of Tibetan languages*. Ed. by Lauren Gawne and Nathan W. Hill. Berlin: Mouton De Gruyter, 2017, pp. 61–94.

Gong, Qun Hu. *Zhabayu yanjiu [A study of nDrapa]*. Beijing: The Ethnic Publishing House, 2007.

Hagège, Claude. "Les pronoms logophoriques". In: *Bulletin de la Societé de Linguistique de Paris* 69 (1974), pp. 287–310.

Hale, Austin. "Person markers: Finite conjunct and disjunct verb forms in Newari". In: *Papers in Southeast Asian Linguistics No.7*. Ed. by S. A. Wurm. Canberra: Pacific Linguistics, the Australian National University, 1980, pp. 95–106.

Hargreaves, David. "Agency and intentional action in Kathmandu Newar". In: *Himalayan Linguistics* 5 (2005), pp. 1–48. doi: 10.5070/H95022977.

Hill, Nathan W. and Lauren Gawne. "The contribution of Tibetan languages to the study of evidentiality". In: *Evidential systems of Tibetan languages*. Ed. by Lauren Gawne and Nathan W. Hill. Berlin: Mouton De Gruyter, 2017, pp. 1–38.

Honkasalo, Sami. "A grammar of Eastern Geshiza". PhD thesis. University of Helsinki, 2019.

Huang, Bu Fan. "Muyayu gaikuang [An outline of Munya]". In: *Minority Languages of China* 3 (1985), pp. 62–77.

Huang, Bu Fan. "Zhabayu gaikuang [An outline of nDrapa]". In: *Journal of the Central University for Nationalities (Human and Social Sciences Edition)* 4 (1990), pp. 71–82.

Huang, Bu Fan. *Lawurongyu yanjiu [A study of Lavrung]*. Beijing: The Ethnic Publishing House, 2007.

Huang, Bu Fan and Wang Mu Renzeng. "Shixingyu [Shǐxīng]". In: *Zangmianyu shiwuzhong [Fifteen Tibeto-Burman languages]*. Ed. by Qing Xia Dai et al. Beijing: Beijing Yanshan Press, 1991, pp. 174–197.

Huang, Bu Fan and Fa Cheng Zhou. *Qiangyu yanjiu [A Study of Qiang]*. Chengdu: Sichuan People's Publishing House, 2006.

Huang, Cheng Long. "A reference grammar of the Puxi variety of Qiang". PhD thesis. City University of Hong Kong, 2004.

Huang, Yang. "Egophoricity in nDrapa". In: *52nd International Conference on Sino-Tibetan Languages and Linguistics* [Paper Presentation]. The University of Sydney. Sydney, June 2019.

Huang, Yang. "Zhabayu de shizheng fanchou [The evidential categories in nDrapa] [Paper Presentation]". In: *Fifth Workshop on Sino-Tibetan Languages of Southwest China*. Nankai University. Tianjin, Aug. 2019.

Hyslop, Gwendolyn. "Evidentiality in Bodic languages". In: *The Oxford handbook of evidentiality*. Ed. by Alexandra Y. Aikhenvald. Oxford: Oxford University Press, 2018, pp. 595–609.

Jacques, Guillaume. *Jiarongyu yanjiu* [*Study on the Rgyalrong language*]. Beijing: The Ethnic Publishing House, 2008.

Jacques, Guillaume. "Rgyalrong Language". In: *Encyclopedia of Chinese Language and Linguistics*. Ed. by Rint Sybesma et al. Leiden: Brill, 2017, pp. 583–589.

Jacques, Guillaume. "Egophoric marking and person indexation in Japhug". In: *Language and Linguistics* 20.4 (Sept. 2019), pp. 515–534. doi: 10.1075/lali.00047.jac.

Jacques, Guillaume et al. "Stau (Ergong, Horpa)". In: *The Sino-Tibetan languages*. Ed. by Graham Thurgood and Randy J. LaPolla. New York: Routledge, 2017, pp. 597–613.

Jiang, Li. *A grammar of Guìqióng: A language of Sichuan*. Leiden: Brill, 2015.

Jiang, Ying. *Dayang Pumiyu cankao yufa* [*Reference grammar of Dayang Pumi*]. Beijing: China Social Sciences Press, 2015.

Jiang, Ying. "Pumiyu shizheng fanchou diyu chayi de chengyin fenxi [Three possible causes for the geographic variation of the evidentiality of the Pumi language]". In: *Journal of Yunnan Normal University* 51.3 (2019), pp. 44–51.

Lai, Yun Fan. "Grammaire du khroskyabs de Wobzi [A grammar of Wobzi Khroskyabs]". PhD thesis. New Sorbonne University Paris 3, 2017.

LaPolla, Randy J. "Evidentiality in Qiang". In: *Studies in evidentiality*. Ed. by Alexandra Y. Aikhenvald and R. M. W. Dixon. Amsterdam/Philadelphia: John Benjamins Publishing Company, 2003, pp. 63–78.

LaPolla, Randy J. and Cheng Long Huang. *A grammar of Qiang: With annotated texts and glossary*. Berlin: Mouton de Gruyter, 2003.

Lidz, Liberty A. "Evidentiality in Yongning Na (Mosuo)". In: *Linguistics of the Tibeto-Burman Area* 30.2 (2007), pp. 45–87.

Lin, Xiang Rong. *Jiarongyu yanjiu* [*A Study of rGyalrong*]. Chengdu: Sichuan Nationality Press, 1993.

Lin, You-Jing. "Tense, aspect, and modality inflection in the Zhuokeji rGyalrong verb". MA thesis. Taiwan: National Tsing Hua University, 2000.

Lin, You-Jing. "Tense and aspect morphology in the Zhuokeji rGyalrong verb". In: *Cahiers de linguistique—Asie orientale* 32 (2003), pp. 245–286.

Lin, You-Jing and Er Wu Luo. "The directional prefixes and verb stem alternations in the Dazang variety of Japhug rGyalrong". In: *Minority Languages of China* 4 (2003), pp. 19–29.

Liu, Guang Kun. *Mawo qiangyu yanjiu* [A study of Mawo Qiang]. Chengdu: Sichuan Nationalities Press, 1998.

Lu, Shao Zun. *Pumiyu fangyan yanjiu* [Studies on the dialects of Pumi]. Beijing: The Ethnic Publishing House, 2001.

Nagano, Yasuhiko. "Cogtse Rgyalrong". In: *The Sino-Tibetan languages (2nd ed.)* Ed. by Graham Thurgood and Randy J. LaPolla. New York: Routledge, 2017, pp. 572–596.

Oisel, Guillaume. "Re-evaluation of the evidential system of Lhasa Tibetan and its atypical functions". In: *Himalayan Linguistics* 16 (2017), pp. 90–128.

Post, Mark. "Person-sensitive TAME marking in Galo: Historical origins and functional motivation". In: *Functional-historical approaches to explanation: in honor of Scott Delancey*. Ed. by Tim Thornes et al. Amsterdam: John Benjamins Publishing Company, 2013, pp. 107–130.

Prins, Marielle. "A web of relations: A grammar of Rgyalrong, Jiaomuzu (Kyom-kyo) dialects". PhD thesis. Leiden University, 2011.

San Roque, Lila, Simeon Floyd, and Elisabeth Norcliffe. "Evidentiality and interrogativity". In: *Lingua* 186–187 (2017), pp. 120–143. doi: 10.1016/j.lingua.2014.11.003.

Sandman, Erika. "A grammar of Wutun". PhD thesis. University of Helsinki, 2016.

Shirai, Satoko. "Evidentials and evidential-like categories in nDrapa". In: *Linguistics of the Tibeto-Burman Area* 30.2 (2007), pp. 125–150.

Song, Ling Li. "Guiqiongyu de jizhong shizheng fangshi [Types of evidentiality in Guiqiong language]". In: *Journal of Changshu Institute of Technology (Philosophy and Social Sciences)* 4 (2018), pp. 49–53.

Sun, Hong Kai. "Qiangyu gaikuang [An outline of Qiang]". In: *Studies of the Chinese Language* 12 (1962), pp. 561–571.

Sun, Hong Kai. *Qiangyu jianzhi* [A Compendium of Qiang]. Beijing: The Ethnic Publishing House, 1981.

Sun, Hong Kai. "Liujiang liuyu de minzu yuyan jiqi xishu fenlei—jianshu jialingjiang shangyou, yaluzangbujiang liuyu de minzu yuyan [The nationality languages in the six valleys and their language branches]". In: *Journal of Nationality Studies* 3 (1983), pp. 99–273.

Sun, Hong Kai. *Zangmian yuzu qiangyuzhi yanjiu* [A Study of the Qiangic Branch of Tibeto-Burman Languages]. Beijing: China Social Science Press, 2016, p. 579.

Sun, Jackson T.-S. "Evidentials in Amdo Tibetan". In: *The Bulletin of the Institute of History and Philology, Academia Sinica* 64 (1993), pp. 945–1001.

Sun, Jackson T.-S. "Parallelisms in the verb morphology of Sidaba rGyalrong and Lavrung in rGyalrongic". In: *Language and Linguistics* 1 (2000), pp. 161–190.

Sun, Jackson T.-S. "Stem alternations in Puxi verb inflection: Toward validating the rGyalrongic subgroup in Qiangic". In: *Language and Linguistics* 1 (2000), pp. 211–232.

Sun, Jackson T.-S. "Tshobdun Rgyalrong". In: *The Sino-Tibetan languages (2nd ed.)* Ed. by Graham Thurgood and Randy J. LaPolla. New York: Routledge, 2017, pp. 557–571.

Sun, Jackson T.-S. "Evidentials and person". In: *The Oxford handbook of evidentiality*. Ed. by Alexandra Y. Aikhenvald. Oxford: Oxford University Press, 2018, pp. 47–63.

Sun, Jackson T.-S. "The ancestry of Horpa: Further morphological evidence". In: *Journal of Chinese Linguistics Monograph Series: The Ancestry of the Languages and Peoples of China* 29 (2019), pp. 24–43.

Sun, Jackson T.-S. "Understanding Tibetic evidentials: New evidence from Sichuan [Paper Presentation]". In: *Fifth Workshop on Sino-Tibetan Languages of Southwest China*. Nankai University. Tianjin, Aug. 2019.

Tian, Qian Zi. "Gexi huoeryu de qingmao fanchou [The verbal modality in Gexi Horpa]". In: *Journal of Sino-Tibetan Linguistics* 11 (2019), pp. 80–95.

Tian, Qian Zi and Jackson T.-S. Sun. "Gexi huoeryu dongci de shi yu ti [On tense and aspect in the Gexi Horpa verb]". In: *Language and Linguistics* 20.3 (June 2019), pp. 451–468. doi: 10.1075/lali.00040.tia.

Tournadre, Nicolas. "La déixis en Tibétain: Quelques faits remarquables [The deixis in Tibetan: Some remarkable facts]". In: *La Deixis*. Ed. by M.-A. Morel and L. Danon-Boileau. Paris: PUF, 1992, pp. 197–208.

Tournadre, Nicolas. *L'ergativité en Tibétain moderne: Approche morphosyntaxique de la langue parlée [Ergativity in modern Tibetan: A morphosyntactic approach to spoken language]*. Paris/Leuven: Peeters, 1996.

Tournadre, Nicolas. "Argument against the concept of 'conjunct'/'disjunct' in Tibetan". In: *Chomolangma, Demawend und Kasbek. Festschrift für Roland Bielmeier zu seinem 65 Geburtstag*. Ed. by Brigitte Huber, Marianne Volkart, and Paul Widmer. Halle: International Institute for Tibetan and Buddhist Studies, 2008, pp. 281–308.

Tournadre, Nicolas and Konchok Jiatso. "Final auxiliary verbs in literary Tibetan and in the dialects". In: *Linguistics of the Tibeto-Burman Area* 24 (2001), pp. 49–111.

Tournadre, Nicolas and Randy J. LaPolla. "Towards a new approach to evidentiality". In: *Linguistics of the Tibeto-Burman Area* 37 (2014), pp. 240–263.

Watters, Stephen A. "A grammar of Dzongkha (dzo): Phonology, words, and simple clauses". PhD thesis. Rice University, 2018.

Widmer, Manuel. "A descriptive grammar of Bunan". PhD thesis. University of Bern, 2014.

Willett, Thomas. "A cross-linguistic survey of the grammaticization of evidentiality". In: *Studies in Language* 12.1 (Jan. 1988), pp. 51–97. doi: 10.1075/sl.12.1.04wil.

Willis, Christina Marie. "A descriptive grammar of Darma: An endangered Tibeto-Burman language". PhD thesis. The University of Texas at Austin, 2007.

Yliniemi, Juha. "A descriptive grammar of Denjongke (Sikkimese Bhutia)". PhD thesis. University of Helsinki, 2019.

Zhang, Si Hong. "A reference grammar of Ersu: A Tibeto-Burman language of China". PhD thesis. James Cook University, 2013.

Zhang, Si Hong. "The expression of knowledge in Ersu". In: *The grammar of knowledge*. Ed. by Alexandra Y. Aikhenvald and R. M. W. Dixon. Oxford: Oxford University Press, 2014, pp. 132–147.

Zheng, Wu Xi. "A grammar of Longxi Qiang". PhD thesis. National University of Singapore, 2016.

Index

ablaut   13n3, 25
actor   8, 21, 31–33, 35, 40
   first person   31–32, 67–68
      non-volitional   68
      volitional   67–68
   third person   41
addressee   9, 22, 25, 27n13, 49, 51, 59
affix   15, 20n8
affixation   33
agglutinative   6
alterphoric   68, 70
animate   31
aspect   8, 12, 16, 33, 34n14, 51
   durative   59
   egophoric   52n15
   immediate   34, 37
   imperfect   48
   imperfective   69
   marker   47
   non-perfective   69–70
   perfect   45, 62, 70
   perfective   20, 43, 53, 62, 64, 70
   progressive/prospective   69
   progressive-inchoative   52, 69
   prospective   37
   resultative   59
   system   7

binary system   7
Brazilian Portuguese   69

case marker   6
causative directive   59, 69
Chinese
   Mandarin   4
      Southwestern   4
clause   3, 9, 15, 23, 42, 48, 51, 52n15

complement   48, 55
declarative
   second person   46
   embedded   43
   imperative   49
   interrogative   49
   main   3
   matrix   43, 48
   negative   49
   past tense   20
   perfective   27
clause final particle   40–41, 45, 63
Cogtse   12–15, 22n10, 60
command   6
complementizer   69
conjunct/disjunct   43
consonant   4
   bilabial stop   63
   cluster
      initial   6
   prenasalized   6

Dayang. *See* Pumi   54
Dazang   19, 20n6
declarative   3, 7
dialect   2, 4, 10, 12, 30, 33, 40, 53
directional-cum-tense/aspect   12
disjunct   43
dual   4, 17

egophoric   2, 8–9, 15n4, 21, 27, 43, 70
   marker   68
   narrow scope   48
   wide scope   48
egophoricity   2–3, 6–7, 8n1, 9–10, 54, 68–69
endopathic   6, 8, 26, 66, 68

equative copula   15n4
ergative   48
Ergong. *See also* Horpa   12
Ersu   3, 11, 49–52, 63
    Lizu   49, 52, 60, 69
    Proper   49, 52, 60, 66n20, 69
    Tosu   49
evidential   2, 7–11, 15n4, 16, 17n5, 20, 22, 24, 27–30, 33, 41, 45, 49, 51, 53–56, 59, 62–65, 67, 69
    assumed   11, 33, 37–38, 60
    auditory   11, 55–56, 60
    canonical   25
    category   2, 9–11, 58
    construction   57
    definition   39
    direct   1, 3, 6, 11–12, 20, 22–23, 26–28, 38, 40–41, 43, 45–49, 51, 60, 64–68, 70
        Qiangic   66n20, 67
        Tibetic   66n20, 67
        unmarked   66n20
        zero-marked   41, 49
    direct   17n5, 52n15, 66n20
    ego-oriented   27
    egophoric   21
    egophoric/heterophoric   39
    experienced auditory   57
    experiential   20n6
    factual   12, 21, 43
    firsthand   7, 12–16, 20, 23, 26–27, 53, 60
        zero-marked   12
    function   12, 13n3, 23, 25, 53, 62, 64
    gnomic auditory   58
    hearsay   39, 55, 58
    indirect   20n6, 26
    inferential   1–2, 7–9, 11, 23, 26–35, 38–52, 55–56, 60, 62–65, 67, 70
        marker   36, 42, 46–49, 52–53, 62, 70
        incipient   25
        meaning   62
        mirative   39
    non-direct   16, 49
    non-egophoric imperfective   55
    non-experiential   20nn6–7
    non-firsthand   7, 9, 11–17, 19–21, 23, 25–27, 47, 53, 60, 64–65, 67
        imperfective   21
        perfective   20
    non-visual   9, 47
    non-visual sensory   2, 43

observational   11–12, 15, 17–19, 22n10
predictive   11, 33, 36–37, 60
quotative   1–2, 7, 11–12, 27, 29, 40, 43, 48–49, 51, 53n18, 54, 60, 65–66, 69
reportative   27
reported   1–2, 7, 9–12, 15, 17, 20–21, 23–24, 29–30, 32–33, 36, 38–43, 45, 47–49, 51–55, 57–58, 60, 65–66, 69–70
    experienced   57–58, 69
    gnomic   58–59, 69
    marker   50
reported and/or quotative   1, 3, 70
reported thought   55
reported-cum-quotative   52, 60, 69
sense   25, 47
sensory   21–22, 26–27
strategy   55
suffix   29
system   1, 3, 7, 10–12, 15, 26, 55, 59–60, 62, 65
unmarked   66n20
value   52n15
visual   1–2, 8, 11, 30–33, 38–39, 43, 55, 57–58, 60, 65–67, 70
    unmarked   38
    zero-marked   55
zero-marked   10
evidentiality   1–3, 6–12, 15, 17, 19–20, 23, 25, 27, 30–31, 33, 38, 40, 45, 48–49, 52n15, 54–55, 57n19, 58–60, 64–66
    double marking   40
    fused   8
    grammatical   6
    system   10, 30, 60, 64, 70
exclusive   4
existential verb   6
expectation   2

first person   13–15, 19, 23, 26, 28–29, 35, 37–38, 48, 51, 67
firsthand   1, 8, 11, 13
first-person effects   6, 8, 11, 15, 24, 29–30, 35, 47, 53, 65, 67
functional scope   3

Geshiza. *See* Horpa   12
Gexi. *See* Horpa   26
grammaticalization   57, 60, 62, 69
    path   62, 64–65, 66n20

grammaticalize   21, 25, 27n13, 29, 32, 38, 51, 53, 58–59, 65, 69–70
Guiqiong   3, 11, 57, 60, 69

Horpa   11–12, 26
　Central   26
　Eastern   26
　Geshiza   12, 26–27, 29, 60, 63–66
　Gexi   26
　Northern   26
　Northwestern   26
　Rtau   12, 26–27, 60, 64, 66
　variety   62
　Western   26

imperative   13
imperfect   47
　marker   48
imperfective   20, 53, 69
　non-egophoric   57, 69
　non-past   12
　past   12, 20
　past tense   22
inclusive   4
interrogative   7, 56
intersubjectivity   27n13
intransitive   20n8

Japhug   11–12, 17n5, 19, 21, 23, 56, 60
Jiaomuzu   10–12, 15–17, 19, 60

Kamnyu   19–20, 65–66
Khroskyabs   6, 11–12
　Core   23
　dialect   23
　evidentiality   23
　Njorogs   23
　Siyuewu   23
　Wobzi   12, 23–25, 60, 64
Kyom-kyo. See also Jiaomuzu   15

Lavrung. See also Khroskyabs   12
Lizu. See Ersu   49
Longxi. See Qiang   30
Mätro. See nDrapa   41

mediative   12
mirative   9
　effect   54
　extension   11, 31

　function   65
　marker   59
　meaning   26
　overtone   9, 30, 65
　reading   56
　sense   18, 23–24, 33
mirativity   2, 6, 9, 17, 23, 29, 31, 33, 35, 65–66
modality   2, 7, 33, 34n14
　epistemic   2, 10, 63–64
mood   58
　assumed   41
　epistemic   70
　experiential   41
　hearsay   41
　inferential   41
　non-experiential   41
　speculative   58
　system   7
morphology   6, 23
　TAME   21n9
　verbal   26
Munya   3, 6, 11, 15n4, 45, 48, 60, 62–67, 69
　Eastern   45
　Northern   45
　Southern   45
　Western   45

Namuyi   11
nDrapa   3, 11, 40, 42–43, 60
　Lower   40, 43, 66n20
　Mätro   41
　Upper   40–41, 66n20
negator   56
Niuwozi. See Pumi   53
Njorogs. See Khroskyabs   23
non-egophoric   43
non-firsthand   1, 11, 13, 65
non-first person   13–15, 19, 43
non-past   12, 17, 23, 26
non-perfective   69
non-singular   46
non-verbal   2
non-volitionality   17, 33
noun   4
numeral classifier   6

other-person   54

past   13, 15, 17, 26–27
perfect   47, 63

perfective   20, 27, 34, 40, 53, 64
  immediate   34
  marker   43, 52
  past   12, 20
  present tense   22
  third person   41
perfectivity   6
person   7, 11, 51
  marking   33, 40, 48
person-number   6
  inflection   46
  marking   16
phonological reduction   57
phonological word   4
phonology   6, 23
pitch-accent   13n3
plural   4
  marker   6
  third person   16
polarity   7
predicate   3, 20n8
  endopathic   8
  non-volitional   43, 46, 48, 67
  verbal   8
  volitional   46–47
  volitionality   7
prefix   6, 13–14, 19–20, 22, 24
  directional   6, 11–13, 19–20, 25, 34, 53, 56, 64
    non-specific   25
  directional   20n7
  indirect perfect   19
  interrogative   6, 45
  negative   6, 45
  past tense   26
  verbal   12, 69
  vocalic   20n7
prefixal   6
prefixation   13n3
Prinmi. *See also* Pumi   53
pronoun   4
  logophoric   42
Pumi   3, 11, 53
  Dayang   54
  Niuwozi   53, 60, 65
  northern   53–54, 69
  southern   53, 69
  speakers   4
  Wadu   11, 53–56, 60, 63, 65, 68
Puxi. *See* Qiang   30

Qiang   1, 3, 8, 11, 30, 66, 70
  Longxi   30, 39–40, 60
  Mawo   30, 63
  northern   30
  Proto-   60, 62–65
  Puxi   30, 38, 60
  Qugu   11, 30, 33–35, 37, 60, 65
  Ronghong   30–31, 39–40, 56, 60, 65, 67
  southern   30
  speakers   4
  Taoping   30
  type   70
  variety   11, 60, 69
Qiangic
  branch   3
  group   6
  languages   1–4, 6–8, 10–12, 30, 60, 62–66, 68–70
  middle   6
  northern   6
  southern   1, 6, 11, 69
  southern type   70
Queyu   11
Qugu. *See* Qiang   11

reciprocal   6
Rgyalrong   8, 11
  Core   11–12, 25–26, 64–65
  dialect   25
  group   6
  languages   6–7, 21n9
  type   70
Rgyalrongic group   70
Rgyalrongic languages   3, 11–12, 41, 60, 64, 69
Ronghong. *See* Qiang   30
root
  verb   37–38
Rtau. *See* Horpa   12

second person   35, 51
  singular   19
self-person   54–55
sensory   2
sentence final particle   21
Shixing   11, 59
Showu. *See also* Zbu   12
singular   4
  first person   32, 46
  second person   46
Situ   10–12, 15

Siyuewu. *See* Khroskyabs 23
South American Spanish 69
speaker 2, 7–9, 13–14, 15n4, 16–19, 22–23, 25, 27–28, 31, 33, 38, 42, 45, 47, 50–52, 57, 59, 66–67
   native 46
Stau. *See also* Horpa 12
stem alternation 12, 15
stress 16
subject 8, 14, 20n8, 43
   first person 20–21, 23, 28, 46–48
   generic 36
   person 46
   second person 20
   third person 48
suffix 20, 27, 29, 31, 37–38, 41–42
   aspect 35, 37
   mood 41
   person 35, 37
   person-number 36
   verbal 30, 33
suffixation 6
syllable 4, 15
   initial 20n8

Tangut 4, 11
tense 8, 12, 14, 16
   future 12–13
   gnomic 58–59, 69
   non-past 7, 25, 28, 69–70
   past 1, 7, 11–15, 20, 23, 60, 62–64, 70
   present 12–14, 21, 58, 69
   system 7
tense-aspect 12, 13n3, 19, 49, 64
   imperfective 12n3
   perfective 12n3
   prospective 12n3
third person 9, 20n8, 26, 32–33, 35, 51
three-term system 7, 30
Tibetan 4, 63
   Amdo 4, 63, 66–68
   areas 23
   Kham 4
   languages 4
   Standard Spoken 66–67
   Taku 67
Tibetanist 2

Tibetic languages 2, 6, 68, 70
Tibeto-Burman 3, 67
   languages 6, 8
Tibeto-Burmanist 1
tone 4, 13n3
Tosu. *See* Ersu 49
Tshobdun 12
two-term system 7

unmarked 11, 27, 43

variety 10–12, 15, 30, 53–55
verb 6, 28–29, 48, 65
   auxiliary 45
   complex 38, 48
   copula 15n4
   dynamic 21n9, 45, 47, 64
   endopathic 8, 22, 67
   existential 56
   motion 46, 54
   non-controllable 55
   non-volitional 8, 35, 37, 41
   of speaking 29
   past form 28
   predicate 46, 48
   root 13, 16–17, 35, 37
   speaking 53
   speech report 29, 40, 58
   stative 20–21, 45, 56, 64
   stem 37
      alternation 19
      bare 21
   stem 13n3, 20n8
   template 6, 27
   transitive 20, 48
   type 51
   volitional 8, 35, 46
vocalic change 6, 12, 15, 46, 64
volitionality 6, 8, 11, 46, 68
vowel 4, 13, 15, 19, 20n7, 37
   high front 62
   low back 63

Zbu 12
zero-form 53
zero-marked 21, 23, 60
Zhuokej. *See also* Cogtse 12

www.ingramcontent.com/pod-product-compliance
Lightning Source LLC
Chambersburg PA
CBHW052135300426
44116CB00010B/1911